Jun 12 — 26th July Movement founded as a clandestine organization, with Fidel as its leader

Jul 7 — Fidel leaves for Mexico to prepare for a popular armed uprising. There he and Che Guevara meet for the first time

★ **1956**

Oct 28 — Ángel Castro Argiz dies in Birán

Dec 2 — 82 expeditionaries, led by Fidel, land on the east coast of Cuba in the yacht *Granma*.

Dec 20 — Dispersed by the enemy, Fidel, Raúl Castro, Juan Almeida, Che Guevara, Ramiro Valdés and six other guerrilla fighters meet up in the mountains and regroup in Cinco Palmas

★ **1957**

May 28 — The rebels capture the enemy barracks of El Uvero, their first major success

★ **1959**

Jan 1 — As his military dictatorship collapses, Batista flees Cuba. Fidel enters Santiago de Cuba

Jan 8 — Following his triumphal progress through the island, Fidel enters Havana. The revolutionary government is installed, with Manuel Urutia president, José Miró Cardona prime minister, and Fidel head of the Armed Forces. Fidel becomes prime minister six weeks later

Apr 15 — Fidel visits United States

May 17 — Agrarian Reform Law enacted

★ **1960**

Feb — Soviet Deputy Prime Minister Anastas Mikoyan visits Cuba. Soviet Union provides credit of $100m and signs agreement to purchase Cuban sugar and supply oil

on Cuba by suspending sugar imports

Aug 6 — Nationalization of U.S. oil refineries, sugar mills and electricity and telephone utilities

Sep 2 — First Declaration of Havana, condemning "the exploitation of man by man and of underdeveloped countries by imperialist finance capital"

Sep 26 — Fidel addresses the United Nations General Assembly for 4 hours 29 minutes and stays in the Hotel Theresa in Harlem

★ **1961**

Jan 3 — U.S. breaks diplomatic relations with Cuba and closes its embassy in Havana

Jan 11 — National literacy campaign launched

Apr 17 — After 4 days of CIA sabotage in Cuba, 1,500 U.S.-trained Cuban émigré mercenaries invade Cuba at Bay of Pigs and are defeated within 72 hours

★ **1962**

Feb 3 — John F. Kennedy orders the economic, commercial and financial blockade of Cuba

Feb 4 — Second Declaration of Havana: "the duty of every revolutionary is to make the revolution"

Mar 14 — Kennedy administration approves the terrorist program "Operation Mongoose" to overthrow the Cuban government

Oct 22 — The Missile Crisis brings the world close to nuclear holocaust. It is resolved by the Soviet Union and the U.S. behind Cuba's back 13 days later

★ **1963**

Apr 27 — First visit of Fidel to Soviet Union

Fidel Castro
handbook

Fidel Castro
handbook

George Galloway

MQP
MQ Publications Ltd

Author's preface

For nearly 40 years I have been an activist—a militant—in the worldwide socialist movement. For me it has been a faith that never died or dimmed—even in the darkest days. I have fought on the streets for that movement, I have been arrested and carried away by policemen and thrown into cells. I have represented the socialist cause in the British parliament—elected five times, almost always against the odds.

I am a practical man. Though I respect the theorists, the observation that theory without practice is blind is always the one that appealed to me most. And, in my experience, when all is said and done, there's always a lot more said than done. That, above all, is why I have been drawn to study and try to understand those who have actually *made* a revolution. Those who heard Marx when he said the "philosophers have merely interpreted the world; the point, is to change it."

Garibaldi's great unification of Italy, Ho Chi Minh's defeat of first French then U.S. colonial rule, the Bolshevikii, Cromwell, Yasser Arafat, the French revolutionists, Gandhi, Nehru and the Indian Congress, the titanic Tito, Chairman Mao—these subjects are my bedside reading. For the last 20 years as a parliamentarian in the House of Commons, I have used every spare moment to learn from the experience of those who have wrested control from an old order and ushered in a new.

Page 2: **Plaza de La Revolución, Havana, July 26 1966**
Framed by the statue of Cuban hero, Jose Martí, Fidel commemorates the thirteenth anniversary of the assault on Moncada Barracks
Page 5: **Fidel, Havana, 2005**

Of course some of these revolutions failed, and all proved a disappointment to some. And for many people, the conclusion is that change will never come, or that if it does it will not be worth the trouble. But for me revolution is a process not an event. And that process will be uneven—one step forward, two steps back, sometimes two steps forward one step back. But always trying to create the conditions in which new men and women will abolish despoliation, war, domination by the strong and their system of exploitation, one by another.

One of the revolutions to which I have been closest has also been one of the most successful. It is Cuba's revolution. The struggle began (in its current phase) more than half a century ago and is still going strong. I realize that it's premature to predict that revolution's final victory—as the Chinese leader Chou en Lai said in the 1970s, when asked about the importance of the French revolution of 1789, "It's still too early to say!"

I have visited Cuba many times, in good days and bad. I have had the great privilege of knowing the leaders of that revolution, or, in the case of those who are dead, of knowing their children, their comrades, their cellmates, their lovers.

Thus when I was asked to write about Fidel Castro I jumped at the chance. At the time of writing Fidel has temporarily ceded power following major surgery. The overwhelming reaction across the world from politicians and ordinary people has been to wish him well in recognition of his extraordinary achievements. This global goodwill contrasts with the gold-toothed right-wing émigrés in Miami and their obscene dance of death. I believe this beautifully illustrated book tells Fidel's story as most people in the world would see it. And I have no doubt it will enrage the Cuban-American right.

Cuba entered my awareness early. As a small boy I pulled the covers over my head and thought the end of the world was nigh. There was an airplane overhead, flying out of the nearby Leuchars base of the British Royal Air force, and the air the night before had been thick with talk of thermo-nuclear war. I had overheard my parents talking in grave and hushed tones about the Cuban missile crisis, in which U.S. President John F. Kennedy and Soviet Chairman Nikita Khrushchev sought to manage a potentially cataclysmic nuclear standoff over the tiny Caribbean island of Cuba, itself led by the then young bearded revolutionary Fidel Castro.

If anything I was with Kennedy, whose picture adorned the wall of my grandparents' house—as it did the homes of most Irish Catholic families—on account of his recent great triumph over sectarian opposition to become the first Catholic president of the United States. I was drawn too to the glamor of the young dynamic court of the new president echoing with fine phrases about liberty and freedom. Kennedy's apparently calm approach to the crisis in which the Soviet Union had placed missiles for the defense of Cuba against U.S. invasion—just 90 miles off the coast of Florida, a state teeming with gold-toothed Cuban émigrés plotting their revenge against the young revolutionaries who had usurped their ownership of a country they had turned into a bordello—was, I recall, much admired by my left-wing mother and father.

Still, war looked more likely than not that morning, and I in my naivete thought the plane overhead had come to deliver the bomb. If it had, it would have meant the end of human life on the planet. The two superpowers armed to the teeth with nuclear arsenals powerful enough to destroy the earth would not have stopped with a tactical exchange of weapons—meaningless so close to the North American mainland. It would have been, truly, mutually assured destruction.

Only later did we learn how close we had come to the end of the human story. Of how Kennedy's calm had been his, almost alone, amidst a crazy cast straight out of the movie *Dr Strangelove*. And much later, after the demise of the USSR, we read the furious protests of the Cuban leadership at the "climb down" by Moscow amidst their legitimate fears of another U.S. invasion of the island.

By this time this schoolboy had pulled the covers off his head and the scales had fallen from his eyes about Kennedy's talk of liberty and freedom. And I had become a friend of and partisan for Fidel Castro and the revolutionary ideals of genuine freedom and liberty for which he stood. And that is what I am: a partisan, for Cuba, for its revolution, for its leadership for its role in the world. The reader should know this is no dispassionate, "on the one hand but then again on the other hand" account.

I believe that Fidel Castro is one of the greatest men of the twentieth century and that he will be remembered and revered. Of course it helps, as the pictures in this book make clear, that Castro, Guevara, Celia Sánchez, Camilo Cienfuegos and their cadre were some of the most handsome revolutionaries who ever took to the stage of battle. In wondering how things might have been if the Cuban revolution instead of being so romantic, had looked like the brown box-suited apparatchiks who ruled much of the socialist world, I always remember the joke that one of the most significant differences there would have been if Khrushchev had been assassinated instead of Kennedy is that Aristotle Onassis would never have married Mrs Khrushchev.

For more than 47 years, in the teeth of the determination of ten U.S. presidents to destroy their revolution the Cuban people, led by the "Maximum Leader," the Comandante, Fidel Castro, have written their country's name and legend in the stars.

They have spread its example throughout the world—an example of a small people overthrowing the yoke of colonialism and foreign domination, attempting to build a new society populated by new men and new women, and sacrificing their meagre wealth and the precious bones of their soldiers and international volunteers so that others—such as the people of South Africa—might also be free.

Their country—once a brothel, casino and drug trafficking terminus for the Mafia, an offshore crime empire for the Gringos—is now the most popular, coolest place on the planet with friends all over the world. According to the normal laws of politics and economics Cuba shouldn't still be standing. Its close allies almost all gone, choked by four decades of U.S. blockade, battered by subversion, terrorism, assassination plots, bribery, browbeating, insult and slander. But the people of this book still stand, despite everything; and their leader, known throughout the world by the single name Fidel, now the longest serving leader in the world, stands tallest of all.

In Cuba once I saw a slogan painted on a wall. It read, "Walker, there is no path—the path is made by walking." But in truth no person in hundreds of years has done more to show the way for humanity to go than Fidel. The images, the inspiration of the first half century of his revolution have lit a path which others one day will follow. Indeed in Latin America today some already are.

In my homeland of Scotland, in the summertime, the mountains are carpeted with beautiful purple heather. It is a sight to behold. But if you look close enough, amongst the thick carpeting, you may come across something more unexpected and even more beautiful. Sprigs of white heather, so rare and so heart-piercingly lovely that people habitually take some and place it in their lapel as a sign of good luck, of hope, for the future. That's what Fidel Castro is for me. A sprig of white heather in the future's lapel.

Above: George Galloway with Fidel during a Cuban television discussion about the propaganda lies of the U.S. empire, Havana, May 24, 2006.

Note: All quotations are from Fidel Castro, unless otherwise indicated.

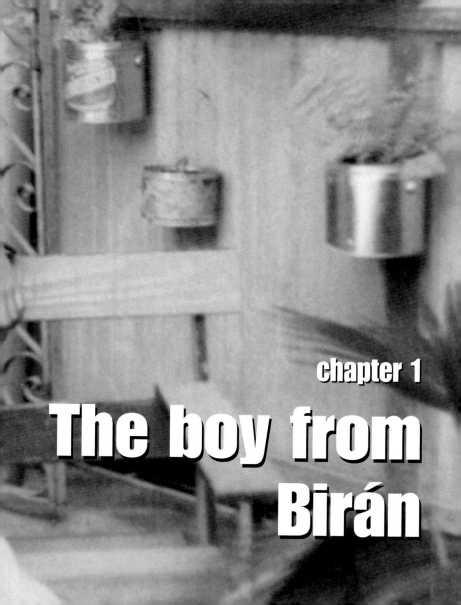

chapter 1

The boy from Birán

A country upbringing 1926–1944

Fidel Castro Ruz was born on August 13th, 1926, on the family farm his father Angel Castro had built up in a remote region of eastern Cuba. The place was called Birán, and it was a couple of hours by road from the city of Santiago de Cuba.

Fidel's mother, Lina Ruz, had already given birth to two enormous babies. The first, Angelita, in 1923, weighed thirteen pounds. The second, Ramón, born in 1925, weighed nearly as much. When Fidel arrived he was twelve pounds. The doctor put these impressive numbers down to the great quantities of fresh milk that Lina drank.

The family home was in the style of Galician houses in northern Spain, from where Angel had emigrated as a young man. It was built on six foot wooden posts, and at night the cows would sleep underneath, alongside the pigs, hens, ducks, guinea fowl, turkeys and geese. It was already a substantial building, and over the years Angel kept adding other buildings—a bakery, a hostel, an inn, a public school, houses for Cuban and immigrant Haitian workers, a dairy, a workshop, a slaughterhouse, a general store, a public post office and a cock fighting pit.

Previous page: **Santiago de Cuba, 1940**
The photograph was taken on the patio of the house of his elder sister, Lidia Castro Argota, when Fidel was thirteen.
Right: **Birán, April 1928**
Fidel in the garden of his house, aged one year and eight months.

I had the opportunity of living among very poor families ... Perhaps those images, those memories and impressions awoke in me a certain sympathy and solidarity toward those people.

Left: **La Casa Birán Mayarí, 1926** Fidel's family home in the year he was born. Although his family was already wealthy, nearly everyone who lived nearby was poor, and Fidel grew up aware of social conditions.

17

Idyllic early years

The vegetation of Birán was lush and tropical; near the house were an orange grove, a banana plantation, papaya trees, coconut palms and some 400 beehives. The young Fidel was a free spirit, by his own account associating the house with the authority he was forever rebelling against, and running all over the countryside with his siblings and friends. They would swim in the river and ride horseback. Often they would eat with the farm workers in their houses.

When he was four Fidel joined Angelita and Ramón in the public school his father had built in Birán, which had some fifteen to twenty pupils. He impressed everyone with his inquisitiveness and was soon reading his favorite epic adventure stories. He was self-assured, impulsive and affectionate, and had an excellent memory.

Left: **Birán, 1929**
Fidel (right) with his elder sister and brother, Angela María and Ramón Eusebio.

Two unhappy years

The rural idyll came to an abrupt halt when, at the age of six, Fidel was sent off with Angelita to live at the house in Santiago de Cuba of the Birán schoolmistress, Eufrasita, who persuaded Angel and Lina that the children would get a better education there. Eufrasita charged the considerable sum of forty pesos for each of them per month, and for Ramón too when he joined them later. She lived with her two sisters, and they provided Fidel, Angelita and Ramón neither with education nor even with decent meals.

I was taken from a world without any material problems and taken to a city where I lived poorly and was hungry ... I was poor because the teacher's family was poor. She was the only one earning any money. That was during the economic crisis of the thirties.

Angelita's attempts to write to her parents to alert them to what was going on were intercepted. Fidel finally escaped with Ramón to become a boarder at the La Salle school in Santiago de Cuba only after arguing violently with Eufrasita and her sisters, after two years in their house.

Right: **Santiago de Cuba, 1936**
Ramón, childhood friend Cristobál Boris, Fidel and, seated, Raúl. Taken while the brothers were at the La Salle College. Fidel was ten years old.

I was a rebel of many causes, and I am grateful for the life I have led, throughout all these years, as a rebel. Even today, and with more reason ... because I understand much better this land in which we were born and this world in which we live.

Left: **Birán, 1937**
Fidel is seated on his father's tractor.

New school, new start

Once Fidel got away to La Salle college, life suddenly changed. He learned baseball and became an expert pitcher. He enjoyed running, swimming and fishing, trips to the mountains and sailing in the bay of Santiago de Cuba. His brother Raúl, who was five years younger, joined Fidel and Ramón at La Salle, and on Sundays the three brothers would visit Angelita at her school for girls.

Fidel recalls being victimized by Brother Bernard, one of his teachers, who hit him on several occasions. Eventually the eleven year old Fidel snapped, threw himself at the teacher and bit his arm. He was sent back to Birán; but he was not content to be out of school and threatened his parents that he would burn the house down if he were not allowed to return to La Salle. They relented.

Angelita was preparing for the final year of high school with a black Haitian teacher called Emiliana Danger. She was impressed by Fidel's quickness and offered to prepare him for the Jesuit college of Dolores in Santiago de Cuba: "She was the first person I met who fired my enthusiasm for something."

At Dolores, a college for the sons of the upper classes, Fidel at first lived in the house of a local businessman who withheld his pocket money if he failed to get the highest grades. Later he boarded at the school. He excelled at baseball, basketball and American football, and spent long days climbing the imposing peaks of the Sierra Maestra, amongst which he would later fight a two year guerrilla campaign. He crammed for his exams rather than study methodically, but did well even so, an approach he continued throughout his school and university days.

During these years Fidel became aware of the reverberations of distant political events. He was nearly ten years old when, in July

1936, the Spanish Civil War, which proved to be the prelude to the Second World War, erupted. Returning to Birán from Santiago de Cuba, he would read the newspapers out loud to the illiterate family cook, Antonio García, who was a fierce supporter of the Republicans. Fidel's father, on the other hand, supported Franco. The partisans of each side would meet together from time to time for an impassioned game of dominos.

In those days Cuban culture was still strongly influenced by Spain, as well as by the economic and technological dominance of the United States. Beyond the private schools, which were in large part staffed with Spanish teachers sympathetic to the reactionary nationalist politics of General Franco, educational opportunities were meager. It was only after he left school that Fidel came into contact with the literature of countries other than Spain.

Next page: **Santiago de Cuba, 1942**
Fidel, aged fifteen, is on the far right, holding the banner of the Colegio Dolores basketball team.

The influence of the United States was strongly felt even in the eastern end of the island, five hundred miles from the capital city of Havana. As a small boy in rural Birán in the 1930s Fidel was familiar with the farms and sugar mills owned by U.S. interests, and the imported machinery and tractors.

While at Colegio Dolores in Santiago de Cuba a U.S. high school team arrived by boat to play a basketball match against his team. Inspired by a great feeling of friendship for the United States, and eager to practice the English he was starting to learn, Fidel wrote a letter the U.S. president, Franklin D. Roosevelt:

I am twelve years old, I am a boy and I think a lot...I do not think that I am writing to the President of the United States...If you like, give me a ten dollars green bill American and I would like to have one of them.

He went on to tell Roosevelt about the mines in the region that could provide metals for building U.S. warships.

Fidel decided he wanted to finish his schooling in Havana, and lobbied his parents to let him go. He was accepted by the Jesuit Colegio Belén, one of the best schools in Cuba, and in September 1942, aged sixteen, set off by train for Havana. Ramón stayed behind to look after the farm, while Raúl continued at Dolores.

Socially Fidel was at first an outsider at Belén among the sons of the Cuban elite, who called him a *guajiro*, or peasant, and he wasn't invited to join the private clubs. Unlike the other students, he made friends among the school servants. As in Santiago de Cuba, Fidel excelled at sports, and in his last year was named high school athlete of the year. He played basketball, football, baseball, track and field. He broke the school records for 200 and 300 meters and for the high jump. He was leader of the school's explorers, and went on excursions to the mountains to the west of Havana at the weekends. He was placed in charge of the school library, where he read until late at night before turning out the lights.

Fidel recalled later of his Jesuit teachers: "I am very grateful to them because they taught me some things that helped me in life, above all, to have a certain fortitude, a certain sense of honor, and specific ethical principles."

St. Thomas Aquinas, whom the Jesuits followed, taught the importance of harmony between idealism and reason. The Jesuits added the ideal of the Spanish *caballero*, of Don Quixote, with his qualities of modesty, tenacity and self-sacrifice. The essentially pre-capitalist moral values of Don Quixote are poorly understood in the Anglo-Saxon world, but in Hispanic cultures Don Quixote is a great hero, as he has always been to Fidel.

At the end of his time at Belén, Fidel's champion, Father Llorente, predicted a bright future for him:

Fidel Castro Ruz has always distinguished himself in everything to do with the humanities. Of excellent character and open spirit, he has been a true athlete, who defended with valor and pride the school's flag. He won the admiration and affection of all. He is now going to study law and we have no doubt that he will fill the book of his life with brilliant pages.

My main activities were sports and exploration. I was in thrall! I had yet to climb the Pico Turquino, and was desperate to do so.

Left: **Birán, Christmas vacation, 1943**

Fidel, aged seventeen, on vacation from his Jesuit college in Havana. He is on a hunting trip with friends. Behind are the mountains of the Sierra Maestra, where thirteen years later he would launch the final struggle to rid Cuba of the Batista dictatorship.

Above: **Havana, 1945**
In the inter-collegiate student games Fidel, aged eighteen, came first in the 800 meters.
Right: **Ecos de Belén, 1945**
Fidel was named best all-round athlete in his school magazine.

A father from Galicia

Fidel's father, Angel Castro Argiz, was born in the Galician village of Láncara, in north-western Spain. His father made carts and builder's tools, and the family lived in a small stone house with thick walls and small windows typical of the region. The cattle and poultry came into the small courtyard at night.

When Angel's mother died after giving birth to her fifth child, the children were sent away to be brought up by their uncles and aunts in a village nearby. This was in 1884. Angel was nine years old.

Galicia was a poor region, which in those years lost many of its sons to emigration. Angel's brother Gonzalo was to emigrate to Argentina. One of his sisters died young. Only his younger sister, María Juana, stayed behind in the family home.

Angel decided early on to try his luck in the wider world. When he was fifteen years old he went to live with an aunt in Madrid, where he found casual work until he was old enough for the army.

Spain at this time was desperately trying to hang on to the remains of its far-flung empire, of which Cuba was the jewel in the crown. Cuba's first war of independence was unleashed by nationalist fighters, known as *mambises*, on October 10th, 1868. Carlos Manuel de Céspedes, a lawyer and small landowner from the east of the island, called for Cuban independence from Spain with the *Grito de Yara*—the Yara Proclamation—and freed his own slaves to fight in the insurgent army.

That first independence war dragged on for ten years. The *mambises* gained control of the eastern and central parts of the island, but were prevented from reaching Havana and the west by Spanish forces which at their peak numbered nearly one hundred thousand men. The truce negotiated at Zanjón in 1878 won unconditional freedom for African slaves and Asian indentured laborers who had fought in the insurgent army, and pledges of political reforms by Spain. But the military leaders of the independence struggle denounced Zanjón as failing to deliver not only national independence, but also the more radical social demands of the movement.

Antonio Maceo, a brilliant leader known with reverence as the Bronze Titan, who came from a humble family of freed slaves in Santiago de Cuba, assembled fifteen hundred men under his command and proclaimed the Protest of Baraguá. They continued the war for a further ten weeks before Maceo, Máximo Gómez and the other military leaders went into exile.

It was at this time that the greatest leader of Cuba's independence struggle appeared on the scene. José Martí was only sixteen when he was imprisoned and then exiled to Spain for political pamphleteering. Still only twenty-six years old, he arrived in New York in 1880 and quickly became the outstanding propagandist for the Cuban Revolutionary Committee during the *"Guerra Chiquita"*—the short war of 1879-80 when General Calixto García led an expeditionary force to Cuba.

In December 1895 Martí launched an invasion of the eastern part of the island. This heralded the start of the war which after three years of bloody fighting finally overthrew Spanish rule. It was the Vietnam War of the 19th century, in which the insurgents faced a Spanish army of three hundred thousand.

Cuban civilians were herded into concentration camps to prevent them supporting the independence struggle, an innovation soon applied by the British against the Boers in South Africa, and later by the Americans in Vietnam.

With the Spanish army in Cuba

In far away Spain, Angel Castro was largely ignorant of the issues animating the supporters of *Cuba Libre.* Not yet twenty years old, the war seemed to provide an opportunity to escape the poverty of his native soil and to fulfil his adolescent dream of a military career. He returned to Galicia from Madrid to join up, but failed to be selected. Undeterred, he offered to take the place of a young nobleman in the army, as was common in those times.

In fact the war failed to resolve anything for the young Angel. He suffered the usual discomforts and privations of a young squaddie, but never saw action. With the end of the war, along with all the other soldiers who had not started families in Cuba, he was repatriated to Spain, a country now bankrupt and in self-denial after the loss of its colonies.

But Cuba had captured Angel's imagination, and he longed to return to its lush landscapes and imagined opportunities. With nothing to hold him in Spain, he made his way back the following year, arriving in Havana on December 4th, 1899 with barely a cent to his name. Illiterate and without skills, he made his way back to the east of the island and found work with U.S. companies that were fast taking control of the economy, in the iron and manganese mines and building railway lines.

Within seven years, now aged thirty-one, Angel had scraped together enough to open a store in the small town of Guaro. Highly energetic, and with an innate talent for organizing others, he began putting together groups of workers for railway building and cutting wood to fire the American owned sugar mills. He took Cuban citizenship and in 1911 he married. The couple had five children, but only two survived.

During the years of the First World War Cuba became a privileged supplier of sugar to the allied countries. Sugar prices rose and rose, and brought prosperity to the mill owners in what became known as the Dance of the Millions. Angel organized gangs to cut and transport cane during the sugar harvests and grew rich. By the time he was forty-five he was managing the estates of former generals of the independence struggle. He bought property, planted sugar cane, forests and fruit orchards, and built up a cattle herd. He had more than 2,000 acres in his own name, and managed at least 25,000 acres in all. Some three hundred men worked for him.

Angel had realized his boyhood dreams. In Birán, a quiet valley with beautiful, lush vegetation that was not even marked on the map, he had recreated a prosperous, tropical version of his native Galicia. But now he was the señor, the benevolent, quasi-feudal lord of all he surveyed. His laborers and their families lived in houses he had built, and he helped them out when work was scarce, and regaled them with exotic foods at the annual festivals. He made his money as middleman from the U.S.-owned capitalist farms, and owned shares in U.S. mining companies, but he wouldn't put his money in their banks and so escaped the inevitable economic crash when it came in 1920.

His wife, however, despised the ways of the countryside and left Angel after seven years. He led a lonely life until, aged forty-seven, he set his cap at the beautiful daughter of one of his sub-contractors, Lina Ruz González. Lina was only sixteen, and her father refused to entertain Angel's approaches. Not only was Lina one-third her suitor's age, but Angel was still married to another woman. Angel took her anyway, although they could not marry officially for eighteen years, when the new Constitution of 1940 made divorce legal.

I grew up in the heart of the family of a great landowner, with all its comforts and privileges, but my father was truly a generous man. We came to understand his way of being and later, on various occasions, we found ourselves resolving problems as he would have done.

Left: **Don Angel Castro Argiz, Birán, early 1950s**

Fidel's father, in his dining room office in the family house. Born on December 4, 1875 in San Pedro de Láncara, Galicia, northern Spain, he returned to Cuba without a penny at the turn of the century, after the end of the independence war.

My mother and father ... were people who worked every day in harsh conditions. They had no social life and hardly any relations with people like themselves. I think that if I had been the grandson or great-grandson of a landowner I might possibly have had the misfortune of acquiring that class culture.

Right: **Birán, July 8, 1925**
Fidel's parents Lina Ruz González and Angel Castro Argiz, one year before Fidel was born. Lina was twenty-two, and Angel fifty. They already had two children, Angelita and Ramón.

Fidel has spoken about his father to several interviewers. By the time he was born Angel was already fifty-one years old, and it was his mother Lina who was closest to the children, providing affection and strict discipline. Angel was by nature taciturn, but a man of strong feelings who commanded great respect. "He was a man of great willpower. He taught himself to read and write, with great effort. Without question he was a very active man, restless, entrepreneurial and with natural organizational abilities."

Fidel also recalls that his father, "like most Galician immigrants, was modest and hard working. Determined and with a strong character. But he was never unjust....There are many witnesses who say he was a generous man. And kind. With a big heart … My father would invent new tasks which were not strictly necessary so as to provide work, even though it didn't make sense from an economic point of view."

Although Angel became a very wealthy farmer and entrepreneur and had a few friends with social position, he never made the transition to being a member of the local bourgeoisie. He was content to remain don Angel, the lord of his quasi-feudal domain. There was something strongly pre-capitalist in his character, which he undoubtedly transmitted to his son Fidel.

Left: **Birán, date unknown**
Don Angel and his large family came to own their own rail car to take them from Birán to the Miranda sugar mill and Santiago de Cuba.

A strong mother

Fidel's mother, Lina Ruz, was born in 1903 in the mountainous region of Las Catalinas in Pinar del Río province, in the extreme west of the island facing the Gulf of Mexico. Her family was poor, making their living transporting goods for others in ox carts.

In 1910, when Lina was seven years old, a terrible hurricane hit Pinar del Río, destroying the tobacco crop, leveling buildings and making the roads impassable. Faced with ruin, Lina's family had little choice but to move to another part of the island and start their lives again. Encouraged by a labor contractor, they took a train to Camagüey province, where they struggled to make a living for the next seven years.

Then, in 1917, her father, don Pancho, met a labor contractor who encouraged him to move on again, to the countryside beyond Santiago de Cuba in the east. The contractor's name was Angel Castro, and his farm was in the quiet valley of Birán. Lina's family packed up their carts and made their slow way east to a new life.

Right: **Birán, April 10, 1926**
Fidel's mother Lina Ruz was born on September 23, 1903 in the small tobacco growing village of Las Catalinas, Pinar del Río province. The photograph was taken four months before Fidel's birth, and is dedicated to friends of the family.

Lina was barely nineteen years old when she fell in love with Angel. After separation from his wife and two children, he had been living a lonely life dedicated to his work for some years when first he noticed her. She was slim, energetic and fearless, knowing how to impose her will. Many have suggested that Fidel owes much of his character to her, noting that throughout his life he has had close relationships with strong women.

Lina, like Angel, had no schooling, and taught herself to read and write as an adult through sheer determination. She quickly learned the skills necessary to run the farm at Angel's side, and developed expertise as a nurse and veterinary surgeon. She rode well and was active around the farm as well as in managing the household. Fidel has remarked that she was a very religious woman, and it has been suggested that her Catholicism, like that of many Cubans, overlapped with the syncretic religion of *santería* which combines aspects of African religions with Catholicism.

Angel left the disciplining of Fidel and his brothers and sisters largely to Lina, and at times she resorted to using a leather belt to bring them into line. Nevertheless, all the children have testified to their affectionate relationship with their mother, and the great respect they had for their father.

Left: **Birán, date unknown**
Lina Ruz dressed for riding.

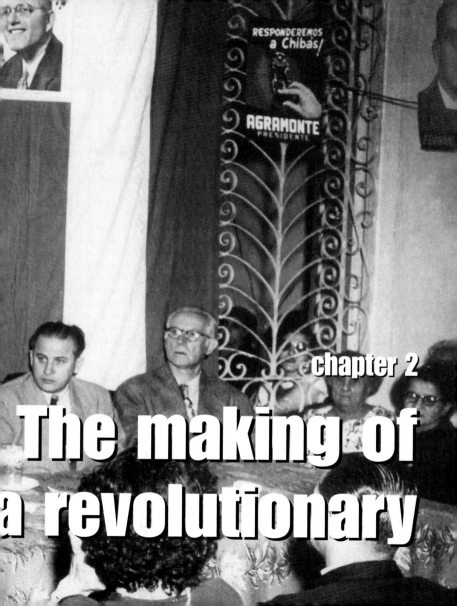

RESPONDEREMOS a Chibás!

AGRAMONTE
PRESIDENTE

chapter 2

The making of
a revolutionary

The road to revolution 1945–1955

Fidel enrolled at the University of Havana in the fall term of 1945. He studied law and was quickly active in student politics, an unruly nursery for the equally volatile Cuban political scene. According to his tutors, he was a talented student, although by his own account he was not much attracted by the abstractions of jurisprudence.

Fidel was elected vice-president of the student union and, after the resignation of the acting president, was appointed to the top position. There are many political activists in the West who have enjoyed a university education and who can hold forth on the campus conflicts they participated in. But there cannot be many who bore a revolver during their student days, as Fidel is reported to have done. It was not an affectation, but simply a reflection of the violence endemic to Cuban political life.

Previous page: **Fidel speaking at a campaign meeting, 1951**
Fidel joined the Ortodoxo (Orthodox) Party in 1947, a party that campaigned against state corruption and was led by Eduardo Chibás until his suicide following a live radio broadcast. Fidel was standing as a parliamentary candidate for Oriente province.

Right: **Havana University gardens, 1945 or 1946**
Fidel with a group of college friends.

The American presence in Cuba

Like so much else in the Cuba of Fidel's youth, gun law and gangland violence was a poisonous legacy of U.S. interference on the island. This state of affairs had been brewing since the end of the nineteenth century, which was when America gained its overwhelming influence in Cuba, as it took advantage of the decline of Spanish power over the island.

Cuba had remained a colony of Spain until 1898. Its struggle for independence was symbolized by Fidel's hero, the legendary José Martí, who was killed in 1895 six weeks after returning to the island to launch a guerrilla struggle. Despite Martí's death, the insurgency grew and wore down the Spanish forces. In the following two years Spain dispatched a staggering 200,000 troops to quell the revolt. Sensing the weakness of the ailing European empire, the U.S., emerging as an imperial power in the Americas and the Pacific, moved to declare war on Spain in 1898.

A powerful section of the U.S. establishment, personified by the early newspaper magnate William Randolph Hearst, whom Orson Welles immortalized in his movie *Citizen Kane*, had already been pushing for America to assert itself in the scramble for imperial influence across the globe. Hearst is said to have replied to one of his journalists who reported that there was a lull in fighting between the Cuban rebels and Spain, "You supply the pictures, and I'll supply the war."

The perfect opportunity came in 1898. That February the U.S. battleship *Maine* blew up in Havana harbor killing 258 sailors. The U.S. authorities prepared a dodgy dossier blaming a Spanish mine for the explosion, and Hearst helped to whip up an orgy of jingoism. The U.S. was at war within three months. The Spanish surrendered and signed over Cuba, Guam, Puerto Rico, and the Philippines to the U.S. on December 10, 1898. Immediately, the U.S. Army moved in and took over the island, building up a new infrastructure of ports, roads, and communications.

In 1902, the United States handed over "control" to a Cuban government; but its method of maintaining power over Cuba then is eerily familiar to us today. The island was only nominally independent—Cuba effectively had a semi-colonial status. This had been enshrined in the Platt Amendment of 1901, an agreement that gave the United States the right to intervene militarily in Cuba.

Meanwhile, vast tracts of ruined land were gobbled up by U.S. investors—so that the United States came to control about three-quarters of the Cuban sugar industry, the heart of the economy.

Soon, Cuba became a playground for the rich. Downtown Havana became a high rise outpost of America, and its luxury hotels housed vast gambling casinos. They were run by professional gamblers and gangsters from the United States who operated hand in glove with corrupt Cuban authorities. Graft was ingrained in every aspect of island life. Havana and Varadero developed into glitzy tourist resorts, awash with casinos, bars, strip-clubs, and incessant gangland infighting.

Violence spread to local politics too—Cuban presidents regularly called on U.S. forces to intervene against their political opponents. A succession of puppet presidents ensued.

Fidel: a leader of student protest

Fidel grew up during the 1930s in an atmosphere of anti-U.S. feeling. He was born two years into the dictatorship of General Gerardo Machado Morales. As for civilian politicians, they were hated for their subservience. Machado was overthrown in 1933 and replaced by a new government under Colonel Carlos Mendieta. Behind him stood the real power, Fulgencio Batista, a former sergeant who, as a mulatto, was himself forbidden to enter the playgrounds of the rich on account of his color.

Batista came to dominate Cuban politics over the next two decades—sometimes directly as president, always as the acknowledged strongman of the establishment. Initial hopes that his coup might lead to progress and an end to tyranny were soon dashed. Batista became a byword for corruption and arbitrary violence.

Fidel, an outstanding athlete at university and skilled student orator, was from that layer of educated Cuban society that desperately wanted meaningful independence and the modernization of the island to replace the system of graft that benefited only the venal few. His inspiration was the legendary fighter for Cuban independence and national development, José Martí.

In 1947 Fidel joined the Partido Ortodoxo (the Orthodox Party), which was dedicated to exposing state corruption and demanding reform. That summer he became part of the Caribbean Legion, a group which attempted to spark a political transformation in the Dominican Republic by sailing there and triggering a revolt to overthrow its equally corrupt dictatorship. Fidel, ready and eager for action, set sail in one of the expedition's boats.

But Cuban President Ramón Grau San Martín sent forces to intercept the expeditionaries. Fidel escaped by jumping overboard and swimming two miles to shore. This exploit ensured his widening reputation among fellow Cuban radicals. Shortly after the failed Dominican expedition he returned to university.

The following year, on 12 October 1948, he married Mirta Díaz-Balart. Their son, Fidelito, was born on September 1, 1949, but the marriage was not to last and the couple divorced in 1955. Mirta was from a wealthy and well-connected Cuban family that left Cuba after the Revolution and settled in Miami. Mirta's brother Rafael is the father of U.S. Congressmen Mario and Lincoln Díaz-Balart, vociferous members of the right wing Cuban political mafia who today are among Fidel's most ferocious opponents in the United States.

From Martí, I received inspiration ... above all ethics ... Marx showed us the idea of what society is and the history of the development of human society.

Left: **Havana University, 1947**
At twenty years old Fidel was Vice-President of the Law School, and leader of a new group he had created called the Student Movement for Caribbean Action.

Next page: **Havana, October, 1947**
Fidel at the front of a demonstration convened by the Federation of University Students to protest the killing of a student.

He always begins in a nearly inaudible voice, quite hesitant, pushing forward in the fog on an uncertain course, but seizing upon any glimmer to gain ground inch by inch, until he lashes out with something like a great paw and grabs hold of the audience.

Gabriel García Márquez

Left: **Havana University, 1947**
Fidel addressing fellow students.

When I enrolled in this university at the end of 1945, we were living through one of the worst eras of the history of our country and also one of the most deceptive. I was actually living through the aftermath of a frustrated revolution, the revolution of 1933. The struggle against Machado had turned into a real revolution.

Right: **Havana, 1948**
Fidel wounded by police while protesting their violation of the autonomy of the university.

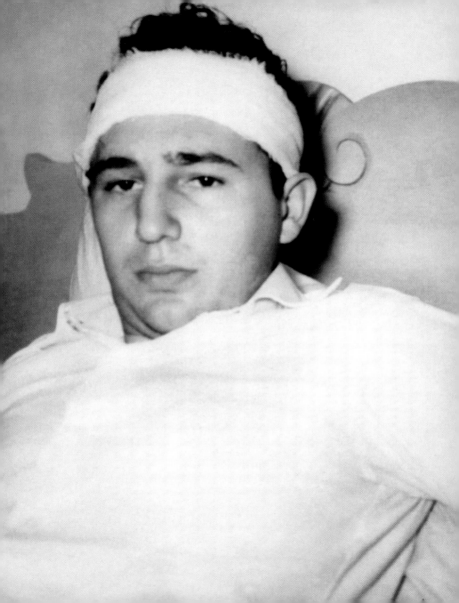

Establishing his authority

In April 1948 Fidel attended a student conference in Bogotá, Colombia. Immediately he was involved in violent political action. The leader of the Liberal Party of Colombia, Jorge Elécier Gaitán, was assassinated, riots broke out and Fidel took part. A truce between the president and the Liberal Party left the Cuban students dangerously exposed, and Fidel's life was for a while in danger.

Fidel graduated in 1950 and joined the law firm Azpiaza, Castro y Rezende, where he spent most of his time offering a free service to the poor. On March 10, 1952 Batista came out of the shadows and engineered a coup. Fidel, a candidate for Congress for the Ortodoxo Party, sent a letter to him predicting that the coup would bring another round of corruption and violence.

He used his lawyer's skills to appeal to the constitutional court to rule against the seizure of power and called for Batista to be thrown in prison. The court rejected the appeal, perhaps injudiciously declaring that "revolution is the source of law." Fidel took the court at its word and began clandestine meetings with other idealistic young men to plan for a different kind of revolution, drawing on the deep insurrectionary traditions of Cuban history.

Left: **Panama, March 30, 1948**
Fidel participated in the Latin American Student Conference in Bogotá, Colombia. He made a side trip to Panama with friends to show support for students there, several of whom had been gunned down while demanding that the United States give back control of the Canal. While in Bogotá, left-wing Colombian leader Jorge Gaitán was assassinated and Fidel found himself participating in an uprising that became known as the "Bogotazo."

In the university, where I arrived simply with a rebel spirit and some elementary ideas of justice, I became a Marxist-Leninist and acquired the sentiments that over the years I have had the privilege never to have felt the slightest temptation to abandon.

Left: **Opposite the Havana University steps, November 1, 1950**
Fidel confronting the Havana police chief during protests.
Next page: **San José, Havana Province, 1951**
Fidel launched a political campaign following the death of Eduardo Chibás, the leader of the Ortodoxo Party.

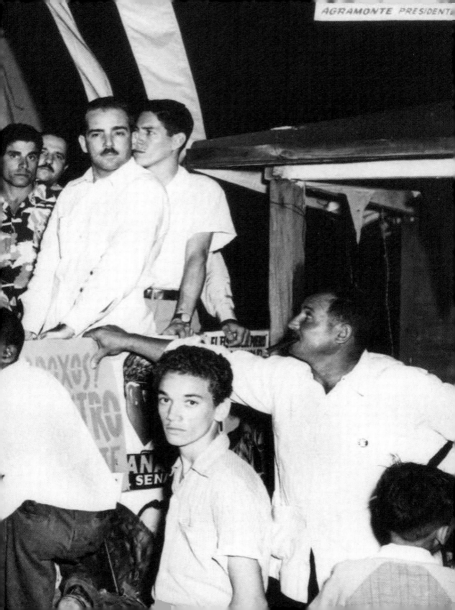

The intellectual author of this revolution is Jose Martí, the apostle of independence

Right: **Vivac central police station, Santiago de Cuba, August 1, 1953**
Awaiting trial for the failed assault on the Moncada Barracks. Ironically, Fidel is pictured beneath a photograph of Cuba's 19th century revolutionary hero José Martí whom, in his speech to the court, later published as "History will Absolve Me," he was to uphold as the inspiration for his revolutionary ideals.

Inspired by Cuban's national hero

Fidel, with his brilliant instinct for symbolism, openly laid claim to the mantle of the great 19th century Cuban revolutionary, José Martí. You could say that he deliberately followed in Martí's footsteps.

Martí was born in 1853 to Spanish immigrants in Havana. A museum near the harbor serves as a physical memorial, while his true legacy is felt across the entire continent. He was still at school in 1868, when the first Cuban war for independence from Spain erupted. The following year this son of a policeman helped publish a newspaper whose radicalism quickly drew the attention of the authorities. Aged just 16, he was sentenced to six years in prison. After six months of hard labor at a stone quarry he was incarcerated on the Isle of Pines and then, in 1871, exiled to Spain.

Martí was able to complete his university studies in Spain and, while specializing in law, was deeply influenced by the progressive educationalist theories that had flourished in Germany in the wake of the great French Revolution.

By 1878, after ten years of fighting, Spain still held the island of Cuba. Martí was allowed to return that year under an amnesty. He threw himself into underground activity but was soon discovered. The following year he was again sent into exile. For the next 15 years he was based in New York, where he tried to unify the fragmented Cuban émigré community. It was during this time that his most far-reaching ideas were forged.

Anticipating the debates that were to rage in the anti-colonial movements of the twentieth century, he asked what the purpose of national independence was, whose interests was it to serve? He saw in Venezuela, Guatemala, and Mexico states that were formally free from their old colonial masters. But in each case the new masters were the military and the big landowners, who enriched themselves at the expense of both the people and the development of the nation. At the bottom of the heap lay the indigenous peoples, who were just as excluded as they had been under Spanish rule.

For Martí, independence had to mean more than a change of flag. As he astutely commented:

The Cuba problem, needs, rather than a political solution, a social solution.

At the heart of that social transformation Martí said that there had to be "mutual love and forgiveness" between the white settler population and the black Africans, who had been brought to the island in chains in the holds of slave ships. Independence in Latin America also required institutions rooted in its soil, not grafted on from an incompatible species.

Martí shared the dream of the father of Latin American independence, Simón Bolívar, for "a great confederation of the peoples of Latin America." So he was implacably opposed to those who wanted to free Cuba from Spain merely in order to annexe it to its northern neighbor, the U.S. In April 1895 he led a tiny band ashore at the village of Playitas on the southern coast of eastern Cuba—just east of a then little known place called Guantánamo Bay. Within six weeks, Martí was dead, killed by Spanish forces in an ambush. Cuba had lost one of its greatest leaders. But he was to have a towering impact on the island's future. As in the lyrics he composed for what became the song "Guantanamera", he was "un hombre sincero," a sincere man, from where the palm trees grow.

Interview with Ricardo Alarcón

HAVANA 25 May 2006

Ricardo Alarcón de Quesada is the President of the National Assembly of People's Power, the Cuban parliament. He was Cuba's Ambassador to the United Nations in New York and remains Cuba's key negotiator in all matters concerning U.S.-Cuban relations. He was a student at Havana University and a member of the Directorio Estudiantil—the Student Directory—when the Revolution triumphed in 1959.

What do you think was uniquely Fidel Castro's contribution to the revolution and to its subsequent development?

I think there are many unique contributions. He will be forever remembered in our history for having been decisive in the achievement of national independence. His role was decisive in uniting not only the various organizations that fought against Batista, but in uniting the people. At the beginning of the revolution we spoke a lot about unity—that meant for us, uniting the organizations and the militants. Fidel always looked beyond that. He was concerned about uniting the people. On one occasion, in a famous speech, he used the phrase "we have made a revolution that is bigger than us." It was a way of saying to all of us that our strategies, perspectives and programmatic views are a minor thing—the revolution is bigger than that and the people are bigger than that. He earned very early the full confidence of the people. He had begun to earn that confidence before the revolution. If you go back to the 1950s, the general environment in Cuban society was one of frustration. Cubans would not normally expect anything from politicians. They didn't believe them. They had been deceived so many times. Together with that was the history of U.S. intervention. I remember talking with friends and relatives who said, "You are crazy. If you advance in a revolution, the Americans will come and invade." They had done that several times.

To overcome the inferiority complex towards the U.S. and to win the confidence of the people was a major achievement. How was that done? In my opinion that was the significance of the attack on the Moncada Barracks. A lot of people, especially the older generation said, "You are going to risk your life; you are going to get killed for others to come to power, steal money and administer the same semi-colony—it's been done before." But they were also impressed that at Moncada Fidel actually did something, rather than simply talk about it. Then later he promised to return to fight. And he did return. He got a reputation for doing what he promised to do. If you follow Fidel's speeches and interviews he is always very keen to tell the truth. Any Cuban would define him as the guy who tells the truth no matter how difficult and hard the truth is.

Then we have the Bay of Pigs. We won against the mercenaries. At that moment the morale of the people was very, very high. Not only did we now have a government of people who tell the truth, people who do their best to accomplish what they said they would do—they are not demagogues—they had managed to succeed against a military attack supported by the U.S. In many other respects Fidel may be seen as making a very important contribution. There is the phase of the revolution we are going through now, after the demise of the Soviet Union—which he anticipated in a speech the year before the Berlin Wall came down. In it he said that if one day the

Soviet Union were to disappear, we would continue the struggle for socialism. Most of the audience didn't understand why he made the reference. Of course, he had information and he knew what was going on. And when the collapse of the USSR did come, he said we are going to overcome this crisis. Now you will find many people still complaining about shortages and so on, but they also feel we have fundamentally overcome that crisis.

If I were to try to summarize one contribution, I would say that Fidel was able to transmit the feelings, motivations, and attitudes of militancy to an entire nation. I remember in the 1960s when the U.S. Students for a Democratic Society was launched. In its manifesto it referred to the main obstacle, the main enemy, as apathy. The students said we have to overcome apathy to make history change. Apathy means, among other things, a lack of sensibility, a lack of commitment.

Fidel's main characteristic is that he is a person whose only fault, his only limitation, is that he cannot do anything half way. The level of his dedication, the commitment I've never seen in anyone else. When he is involved in anything, he will devote body and soul, 24 hours a day, every day. And he does not know how to stop.

That's why he can tell you exactly how many Cuban doctors are in Pakistan, how many are in Guatemala, how many students are in that school—because he was involved in the organization of that group of doctors or that school. He goes completely to the last detail; he will not stop half way. That's why he can be awake the whole night, discussing, talking about things that he is involved in. So we are talking about that sense of involvement, commitment, and militancy—and the other things come from that, that's my impression.

When he moves on to the next fight does he still remember the details of the previous battle?

You can be sure about that. One thing that is noted by everyone who knows him is his memory—his incredible capacity to remember facts and details. He is an amazing observer. But that has to do with dedication and devotion, in my opinion. I have had the experience of spending a long time discussing a particular issue only to then have a discussion about another problem during which he shows the same mastery of detail. He may, on the other hand, in the middle of that discussion ask what day of the week it is or what time it is. It can be half past two in the morning and you have to suggest to him that it might not be a good time to phone a foreign ambassador or dignitary! He works every day. He also has natural qualities of health, to which you can add his discipline and restraint in eating and drinking. He has even gone for many hours without drinking water, or going to the bathroom, or standing up and moving around.

On one occasion I went to the presidential palace for a meeting that began around 4 P.M. and went on all the way through the evening. I had a delegation of Latin American parliamentarians in Havana who I wanted him to see. When I arrived for the meeting he asked me when the MPs were leaving. I said tomorrow midday—so ok, plenty of time. As we entered a second meeting late in the evening, he asked the same question, "When are they leaving?" At some time after midnight he asked what they would be doing. I said they were probably sleeping because it was 3 A.M. The meeting continues towards 7 A.M.. At that point he says, "Let's go and visit the parliamentarians." In the car he asks whether half an hour with them will be sufficient because he feels a bit tired. Well, I felt a bit tired too! I said, "Comandante, for a head of state to have a half hour meeting with some parliamentarians—not even another head of state—and to go to where they are staying to meet them, that's more than sufficient." We arrive there. At about 10.20 A.M. we left and I went to my office to make a phone call and then get to bed. I took a call from a member of my staff. Did I know where the Comandante was? I said he was probably in bed getting some rest. The member of staff said no, he had been in touch and urgently wanted some papers. That day he was due to meet some business people from Europe. I turned on the television around noon and there he was with the Spanish business people.

I met him later in the afternoon and I was absolutely exhausted. He told me he had managed to sleep two hours and was very happy. All I could say is that I too had managed two hours. He has the quality of stamina at a superlative level. Fidel will never retire.

Is there a public Fidel and a private Fidel?

I think there is only one Fidel. The exception is when he is sleeping. Let me tell you another anecdote. I was ambassador to the UN and one day I received a letter from Celia Sánchez, his secretary, asking me to send her, for Fidel, books of North American literature—Faulkner, Henry James, etc. If possible they were to be good Spanish translations, if not, then in English. I began collecting the books and sending them. I wasn't sure what the reason was. Then I remember we were traveling in a plane with some international guests. I waited until Fidel had an empty seat next to him and I sat down. "Comandante, are you receiving the books?" I asked. "Yes, yes, I'm getting them," he answered. He said he was waiting for something by Faulkner. I had only sent him, I think, two parts of a trilogy. So why did he want these books? Answer: he said he met

American delegations from time to time and had realized there was a big hole in his culture—American literature. So he was determined to fix it!

On the question of statistics: another anecdote. He sent a message to say he wanted to meet with me. I arrived and suddenly he referred to a message that I had sent from New York but hadn't addressed to him. I hadn't felt it was so important that it should go to Fidel. It was a note of a conversation I had had with the foreign minister of another Caribbean country. Fidel didn't have the message in front of him but from memory he said that I had written how this country had increased its production from x to y. And Fidel said, "That's not possible. Unless they have some special irrigation system." As he went on I didn't have a clue what he was talking about. But he was intrigued and wanted to know whether there was indeed some new irrigation method. I suspect that the other foreign minister had simply got the figures wrong.

If there had been no Fidel Castro, would there have been a Cuban revolution?

I think so … I think so. It may have not had the exact same characteristics. It may have not been on the same date. It may have been later. I believe personalities play a role in history. But there were other factors and circumstances in Cuba that would have created that personality. In Cuba we had very big personalities in the nineteenth century. For many years at the beginning of the so-called republic in the early twentieth century one of the most popular songs in Cuba was a tribute to the national independence leader José Martí. In a sense Fidel is the Martí of our generation. Martí was a revolutionary and a writer. Fidel is also, by the way, a very good writer. Martí was the organizer of the party that conducted the last war of independence. He was, like Fidel, a very good orator. Another thing they have in common is their devotion and dedication. If Fidel had not existed, the Cuban people would have created him, they would have produced him.

The assault on Moncada Barracks

It was not a putsch designed to score an easy victory without the masses ... It was a surprise action to disarm the enemy and arm the people ... marked the start of action to transform Cuba's entire political, economic and social system and put an end to foreign oppression, poverty, unemployment, ill health and ignorance that weighed upon our country and our people.

Raúl Castro

The assault led by Fidel on Batista's Moncada barracks—a heavily armed Bastille the storming of which would have provided weapons aplenty for the revolutionary cause—has long been recognized as a pivotal moment in the Cuban revolution. At dawn on the 26th of July 1953 Fidel's small band, divided into three units, approached the barracks in the center of Santiago de Cuba as the local santiagueros were still sleeping off a night of Carnival revelry. The events that ensued were to become part of the legend of the Cuban Revolution. Fidel later named his political party the 26th of July Movement, and after the Revolution, the 26th of July became Cuba's national holiday.

Right: **Cuban poster**
Fidel with his younger brother Raúl and, in the background, Che Guevara.
Next page: **Santiago de las Vegas, Havana province, December 5, 1952**
A clandestine meeting held in a small town near Havana. Seated to Fidel's right is Abel Santamaría, a revolutionary leader tortured and assassinated the following year after the failed assault on the Moncada Barracks.

The trigger for Fidel's assault on Moncada was the coup instigated by Fulgencio Batista in March 1952. Batista knew that the election was due, but couldn't be certain of the outcome. His chief potential rival, the popular Eduardo Chibás, was dead, having shot himself on live radio the previous year in a desperate act that showed the depths to which politics in mid-century Cuba had sunk. Still, Batista was taking no chances. The old powerbroker behind various prime ministerial ciphers was not prepared to risk the outcome of an election. And besides, there was a new generation starting to gather forces—among them Fidel Castro.

The debate on whether Fidel intended Moncada to be a bid for political power—i.e. a violent regime change—or the clarion call for a revolutionary struggle to be unleashed by the Cuban people has rumbled on over the years. What cannot be in doubt is that the event has Fidel's fingerprints all over it; and it contains many of the iconic elements of his style that have become so familiar—the complexity of his strategic thinking, his meticulous planning, his exaltation of honor, dignity and self-sacrifice, his extraordinary ability to inspire others, and his total contempt for danger.

When nationalistic junior army officers approached him, Batista needed little persuading to front a coup. Disillusion with grotesque government corruption reached even to the officer corps. As for Batista—better to be at the head of the revolt than to be left behind. So, in the early hours of Sunday March 10, 1952, he drove to the army's headquarters and arrested the senior officers while they were in bed. No one lifted a finger to defend the ailing government of Carlos Prío. A rotten republic died. But Batista, riding the high expectations of those who dreamt of progress, was to achieve only the replication of the worst excesses of the regime he replaced.

For Fidel, Batista's coup was a defining moment. Chibás, the charismatic leader of the Orthodox Party, a man who had cut his teeth as a student agitator in the 1920s and as a radical in the 1930s, was dead. Buried with him was the fiction of progress through corrupted parliamentary channels, which, as Fidel saw only too clearly, were dammed up with gangsterism and chicanery.

As his party collapsed into rival tendencies, and as the space for official politics narrowed, Fidel led the younger members of the Orthodox party towards a new realization of political reality in Cuba. Drawing deep on Cuban traditions, he struck out on the path of revolution. Batista had scraped away the veneer of parliamentary democracy; the only way forward was to bring to the surface a more profound popular sentiment.

Fidel set about a daring plan to instigate just such a popular uprising. Its aim, as he would put it many years later, was "first, to paralyze the activities of the traditional politicians, who were trying to resolve the situation by making deals and arranging a non-revolutionary electoral compromise; second, to lift the people's revolutionary spirit; and third, to gather "the minimum forces required"—i.e. required for a revolutionary breakthrough.

This was the background to Fidel's thinking behind the assault on the Moncada barracks on July 26, 1953. He was later to say that, while the first two aims were strategically correct, there was, in choosing Moncada to achieve the third, no need tactically to make quite "such a noise." In fact his planning was conducted in silence and secrecy—Fidel kept his cards very close to his chest. Such was the intended element of surprise that his brother Raúl himself only learnt where the action was to take place (in the province of Oriente) at the last minute.

Raúl and other comrades "were given their train tickets and saw they were headed for Santiago." With the exception of those who did the driving, the people who traveled by car didn't even know what province they were headed for! In the months running up to the assault, Fidel had quietly rallied support, especially among the younger members of the Orthodox party. By the time of the assault his movement had over 1,500 people organized in 150 cells.

In preparation for the attack Fidel sent ahead to Oriente Province Ernesto Tizol, who rented the Siboney farm, some 30 kilometers from Santiago de Cuba. Arms and uniforms were sent by train and bus in boxes marked as animal feed and agricultural equipment. The guerrilla band was to be reared on what, to the outside world, looked like, of all things, a chicken farm! Fidel later recalled, "We became friendly with the peasant on the farm opposite, and he never suspected anything."

During the days leading up to the attack on the barracks Fidel visited his brother-in-law, Rafael Díaz-Balart, who lived in Oriente province and who had become Batista's deputy Interior Minister. From the conversation Fidel concluded the authorities had no inkling of his plan. Fidel called in 165 recruits for the operation. Only five of them knew the nature of the mission.

The group was split into three separate commandos. Fidel would lead the assault on Moncada, Raúl would attack the neighboring Palace of Justice, and Abel Santamaría the hospital which overlooked the barracks. The two women members of the group—Abel's sister Haydée and Melba Hernández—were originally to stay at the farm. But Fidel yielded to their strong protestations and they were placed in the commando that was to seize the hospital. On the eve of battle Fidel characteristically stiffened the resolve of his forces:

In a few hours you can conquer or be conquered, but in any case, listen carefully, comrades; in any case this movement will triumph. If you win tomorrow, what Martí aspired to will be made sooner. If the opposite should occur, the gesture will serve as an example to the people of Cuba to take up the flag and continue onward. The people in Oriente and throughout the island will be backing us ... here in Oriente we are giving the first shout of "FREEDOM OR DEATH!"

When asked what should be done with any prisoners taken, Fidel replied: "Treat them humanely. Don't insult them. And remember that the life of an unarmed man has to be sacred." Not for the first time such revolutionary morality was not to be reciprocated.

The barracks' defenders had the advantage of terrain—Fidel's forces had to attack uphill. Raúl's unit was able to take the Palace of Justice, but a premature skirmish gave the main force at Moncada time to make good their defense and repel Fidel's assault. That they did with a relish that crossed the boundary into bloodlust.

The assault turned into a bloodbath. Ninety guerrillas were killed. Of those captured, 30 were executed on the first night. On the outskirts of the city of Santiago, 21 prisoners were murdered, many forced to dig their own graves. Fidel and Raúl were among those who managed to escape to the hills, but they too were soon captured. Meanwhile, the Santiago military intelligence seized the opportunity to round up oppositionists, among them communists who coincidentally—and quite oblivious to Fidel's action—were holding a conference in the city that weekend.

Fidel's father, Angel, sensed that his son had organized the attack even before news of his involvement broke. When he learnt that Raúl had also taken part, he asked his daughter Angelita to go to Santiago to seek out an acquaintance from the army and ask him to help save his sons. But the soldier's wife told Angelita that she blamed Fidel for the deaths of various family members who were also in the army. Her husband, she said, was out hunting for Fidel. Angelita and her mother, Lina, then sought to prevail upon General Díaz Tamayo. But, ominously, she again made no progress.

Fidel was finally taken prisoner on the Gran Piedra mountain by Lieutenant Pedro Sarría. His name deserves to be remembered. For he saved the young revolutionary's life by refusing to let his soldiers shoot him. "When they were searching the surroundings and found the other comrades' arms, they were really mad," recalled Fidel in a speech in Venezuela in February 1999:

They had us bound and were pointing loaded guns at us; but no, that lieutenant moved from one side to another, calming them down and repeating in a low voice: "You cannot kill ideas, you cannot kill ideas."

Lieutenant Sarría then refused to hand Fidel over to the commander of Moncada, who would have had him tortured and killed. Haydée Santamaría, who was taken prisoner and shared a cell with Melba Hernández, witnessed what would have befallen Fidel in Moncada. She wrote to the other prisoners describing the fate of her brother, Abel, and her fiancé, Boris Luis Santacoloma. An officer came regularly to her cell stained with blood and boasting of the tortures he was inflicting. One day he told her with a smile that he had ripped out one of Abel's eyeballs with his bayonet.

One of the first public reports of the attack came on August 1 from a journalist on a local radio station who rushed to the police station where Fidel was being held. He asked Fidel what the objectives had been. Fidel "affirmed that the idea was to give back sovereignty to the people, to guarantee campesinos their permanence on the land, to liberate rural people from the threat of eviction and the dead time [the eight months of the year after the sugar harvest when there was no work], to give workers participation in the fruits of their labor, to guarantee rights to small landholders, medical attention to the sick, education for children who lacked schools and teachers, to clean up public administration and make life in the country decent … In short, we have come to regenerate Cuba."

Next page: **Vivac central police station, Santiago de Cuba, August 1, 1953**
Having been caught hiding in the mountains after the assault on the Moncada Barracks, Fidel was first taken for questioning to Vivac.

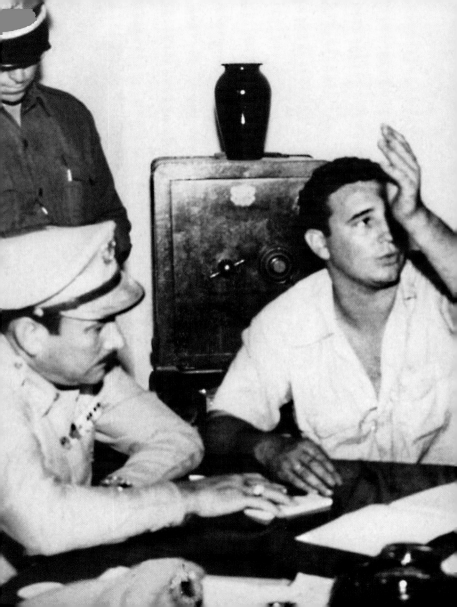

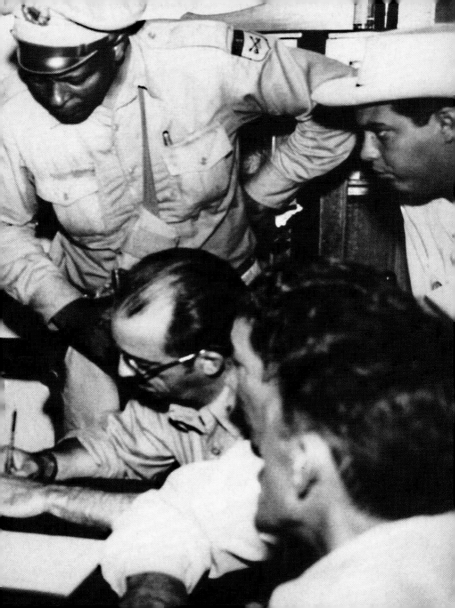

To those of you who call me a dreamer, I quote the words of Martí: "The dream of today will be the law of tomorrow."

"History will absolve me"

Fidel was more than prepared to stand trial for the failed Moncada assault. The dock was just another battlefront for him. His speech from the dock, with its peroration of "History will absolve me," was to reverberate down the decade. He did not hide his involvement in Moncada or his motives when he was captured, taken to the Santiago city jail and interrogated by Colonel Chaviano.

For reasons it is hard to fathom, Chaviano decided to relay Fidel's words to the media and even allowed journalists to interview him, perhaps banking on Fidel condemning himself in the eyes of most Cubans. It was a spectacular miscalculation. Now people could hear from this figure whose name had been buzzing over the airwaves—and they liked what they heard.

Batista's authorities rapidly clamped down. Fidel and the rest of the Moncada veterans were moved to a prison north of Santiago and he was placed in solitary confinement. Press and broadcasting censorship blanketed the island in "a great silence," as the *New York Times* journalist Ruby Hart Phillips put it. Fidel's wife Mirta and his family were not allowed to see him. But he was allowed to write to them after the first two weeks in solitary.

His first request of Mirta was to send two philosophy books by Julián María and García Morente, Shakespeare and "any novels you think would interest me." He added, "Take my blue suit to the cleaners and later send me a shirt for the trial. Keep calm and have courage. We have to think above all else about Fidelito." The distance between Fidel and Mirta was already apparent, as was his devotion to his son. He struck an almost carefree tone in a letter to his brother Ramón a fortnight before the Moncada trial opened on September 21. "For me jail is like a good rest," he wrote. "The only bad thing is that it is obligatory, whether you like it or not—I read a lot and study a lot. It seems incredible, but the hours pass as though they were minutes, and I who am of a restless temperament spend my days reading, scarcely moving at all."

In another letter to Ramón he asked for more boxes of cigars, "because the last one is almost finished, and it is always necessary to give a cigar to persons who help us."

Whether through cigars, his skills as a lawyer, or his charisma, Fidel gained a following among the prisoners held for non-political crimes. Many helped pass secret messages between him and other members of the movement. Fidel was able to organize the legal defense. His strategy was that leading figures and those against whom the evidence of involvement in Moncada was overwhelming should stand by their actions at trial. Those held on suspicion should deny all, and seek acquittal to be in a position to build the movement.

When the trial opened on September 21 at the Palace of Justice in Santiago the chief defendant had partially determined who of the 122 accused was to be found guilty and who would walk free. The three judges were professionals and wanted at least a semblance of due process, so there was a little scope for legal argument. Fidel, conducting his own defense, argued that the uprising had not been against the state and its constitution, but against Batista, who held power unconstitutionally. He declared that Moncada's "intellectual author," the sinister godfather all counter-revolutionary tribunals are desperate to find, was the Cuban nationalist hero José Martí, whose justification of force against tyranny he quoted.

Haydée Santamaría and other defendants gave graphic accounts of torture. For the authorities the trial was in danger of becoming inverted, with the regime and Batista in the dock. Fidel came amongst them not as the accused but as the accuser.

Five days into the trial the prison authorities got two doctors to certify that Fidel was not fit to attend. But he managed to smuggle a note to Melba Hernández who produced it in court, exposing the ruse. An independent medical examination found Fidel to be in perfect health, but that he and the other defendants had good reason for fearing he would be assassinated in prison. The compromise between the court and the army was that Fidel would be tried separately from the rest. The main trial ended on October 5. The assorted anti-regime politicians who had been charged under the "round up the usual suspects" principle were acquitted, as were the rebels whom Fidel had advised to plead their innocence. Twenty-nine of the Moncada veterans were sentenced to between seven months and 13 years.

Fidel's trial took place on October 16 in a nurses' room in the hospital near Moncada—the army still maintaining the fiction that he was ill. The prosecutor spoke for two minutes, saying the defendant had admitted his guilt and should serve the maximum sentence of 20 years. Fidel replied with a two-hour speech that has gone down in history. The text was eventually circulated by his supporters in 1954 after he wrote it down from memory. There's no reason to doubt that it was essentially what he said at his trial: he had kept a fellow prisoner awake for weeks practicing it! He had a formidable memory for such things—indeed for all things—and, in any case, a young journalist took copious notes at the trial.

Fidel began by outlining how the trial had been fixed and his case falsely separated from the rest. "Here was a regime afraid to bring an accused man before the court; a regime of blood and terror … I warn you I have only started … I know that I will be silenced for many years … but my voice will not be drowned. Strength gathers in my heart even when I feel most alone." He told the court of the murder of his comrades. "Some day these men will be disinterred. Then they will be carried on the shoulders of the people to a place beside the tomb of Martí." He said the common soldiers were not his enemy, but were themselves the victims of the dictatorship. He lampooned the claim that his movement had no support, pointing to the 600,000 unemployed, 500,000 farmhands and other sections of society (including the demoralized professional classes) who bridled at the dictatorship. He outlined five Revolutionary Laws that would be the heart of a post-revolutionary order—they ranged from land redistribution, curtailing the freedom of capital, a massive expansion of health and education provision to social housing and reforestation of the island.

His closing remarks invoked a long list of thinkers, including St. Thomas Aquinas, John Milton, and the Jesuit Juan Mariana, and of events: the Glorious Revolution in England in 1688, the 1776 American War of Independence and the French Revolution of 1789, to justify revolt against unjust rule. He closed with the words: "I do not fear prison. I do not fear the rage of the miserable tyrant who took the lives of 70 of my comrades. Condemn me. It does not matter. History will absolve me." When he sat down, the entire courtroom was silent.

Regarding the question of absolution, the speech certainly earned a front-rank place in history. It stands in the radical canon along with John Maclean, the Scottish revolutionary who told his trial, "I stand here not as the accused, but as the accuser"; Eugen Levine, who announced, "We Communists are dead men on leave," and Lenin, who on the day of the victorious October revolution calmly proclaimed, "We shall now proceed to construct the socialist order."

After a four-hour trial and a perfunctory whispered consultation between the judges, Fidel was sentenced to 15 years.

Prisoners on the Isle of Pines

As a student, Fidel had visited the Model Prison on the Isle of Pines in order to denounce conditions there. In October 1953 he returned as a prisoner, with 25 of his followers, to begin his jail sentence. He also embarked on a concentrated period of study. As so often in history, prison for Fidel and his followers was to mean an intense regime of revolutionary education; and it was also to bring personal hardship. On entering Cuba's largest jail he was not to know that he would be released in a general amnesty 17 months later, his political acumen sharpened, the core of his revolutionary leadership forged, and his marriage in ruins.

During his incarceration his reputation as the fiery young leader of the anti-Batista forces grew, as did his political understanding. "The people who run this prison are much more decent and able than those who run Boniato," he wrote to his brother Ramón. "They don't rob or exploit the prisoners like the officials in Oriente … There is discipline here, but no hypocrisy … I don't want to say that we are living in a paradise … but it appears the administration has good will."

Fidel immediately set about organizing his comrades. One of them, Pedro Miret, recalled, "If we were ordered to get up at 6 A.M. we would get up at 5.30 A.M. very well organized." According to Jesús Montané, "From the outset, Fidel told us that our imprisonment should be combative, and we should acquire rich experience from it, experience that would help in the continuation of the struggle once we are freed."

Fidel and the other political prisoners were able to receive books from outside and he set about establishing a library and systematic classes on subjects as diverse as physics, English, literature, history, philosophy—much of them, of course, imbued with politics. He wrote to Natalia Revuelta, to whom he was drawing ever closer, "Every morning at 9.30 and at 10.30 I lecture about philosophy or world history. Other comrades teach Cuban history, grammar, arithmetic, geography, and English. At night I handle political economy and, two times a week, public speaking, if you can call it that." And he read, and read.

His reading list is daunting and eclectic in equal measure. There were the novels: Turgenev's *Home of the Gentry,* Thackeray's *Vanity Fair,* AJ Cronin's *The Citadel, Seven* by Dostoevski, Somerset Maugham's *The Razor's Edge,* as well as novels by Balzac and Victor Hugo. Then there was ancient history, philosophy (Immanuel Kant) and contemporary theory (Sigmund Freud). He read Marx's *Capital,* and great works of history including Marx's *Eighteenth Brumaire of Louis Napoleon* (the famous study of Napoleon III). He read Lenin's theorization of the Bolsheviks' insurrection, *State and Revolution,* and was also taken with *The Secret of Soviet Strength* by Hewlett Johnson, the "Red" Dean of Canterbury, one of many Western intellectuals who were impressed with the Soviet system during the depression-hit decade of the 1930s.

On top of all this, Fidel wrote voluminous letters to political allies outside the prison, and was able to smuggle out the text of his "History will absolve me" speech, which he transcribed from memory. Meanwhile, he was also requesting a large number of lemons! But no one in authority suspected that, like a hero from a boy's own storybook, he was writing in lemon-juice in the white space between the lines of his letters. When heated, the citric acid reacted with the paper and revealed the hidden message. Fidel was determined to keep Moncada and its significance in the forefront of Cuban political life.

My main contradiction is this: I am a man absolutely indifferent to physical or material punishment, with a smile on his lips ... whose only prison ... is his sense of duty

Right: **Isle of Pines prison library, July 3, 1954**
Fidel and his brother Raúl with Fidel Angel, his son from his marriage to Mirta Díaz-Balart, during a visit to the prison where he and his comrades were held after the assault on the Moncada Barracks.

Fidel's letters from prison

Fidel spurred on his friends to seek the prosecution of those responsible for the murder of so many of his comrades. He tried to maintain his leadership of the movement from behind prison walls. Warning against adventurism and amateurism, he wrote, "It is no good if everyone thinks they have the right to make declarations, without consulting anyone. You can't expect much from an organization of anarchic people, each of whom takes whatever path he thinks best."

Fidel wrote regularly to his wife Mirta during his first few months of incarceration. But it was in his letters to Natalia Revuelta that he spoke with emotion and intensity. He wrote to her that love was like a diamond, indestructible, "the hardest and purest of all minerals" but "you can't polish just one facet. It is not perfect until all its edges have been cut and shaped … then it sparkles from every angle, with an incomparable radiance."

His letters to Naty also revealed his deepening political passion. After reflecting on the Haitian slave rebellion and the Paris Commune, he wrote, "I would sincerely love to revolutionize this country from one end to the other! I feel certain that this would bring happiness to the Cuban people. I would not be stopped by the hatred and ill will of a few thousand people, including some of my own relations, half the people I know, two-thirds of my legal comrades, and four-fifths of my former schoolmates!"

Whether by accident or design, the prison authorities managed to send a letter addressed to Mirta to Naty, and one meant for Naty to Mirta. The incident contributed to Fidel's subsequent divorce. Another factor can be laid indirectly at the feet of Fulgencio Batista. The dictator visited the prison on February 12, 1954 to dedicate a new power plant. Fidel and his comrades weren't told who was coming but were told they would not be allowed to leave the hospital wing that day. One of the prisoners managed to spot Batista from a high window. Fidel and the others waited until he was leaving, but still in earshot, and then belted out the revolutionary anthem of the 26th of July Movement.

Batista at first thought the singing was in praise of him. On discovering the truth he petulantly ordered the end of special privileges for the political prisoners and a drastic worsening of conditions. Fidel was placed in solitary confinement. One hundred days into his isolation Mirta wrote to the paper *Bohemia* exposing the conditions Fidel was being kept under.

The letter, and the paper's interest (it named him one of the 12 outstanding world figures of 1953), led to her being sacked from her job at the Interior Ministry. When Fidel heard the news on the radio, he could not believe it—not her being sacked, but having a job in a department of Batista's regime in the first place. He wrote to her immediately: "Perhaps they forged your signature. Or maybe someone has been receiving money in your name. It should be easy to prove. But if this is the work of your brother Rafael, you should demand at once that he take up the matter publicly."

The news that his wife, through her well-connected brother, the Deputy Minister of the Interior, had taken a ghost appointment at the ministry to make ends meet while her husband was in prison struck at Fidel's sense of honor. He wrote to a friend that he could not believe his wife had taken a job with the enemy, "whatever her economic situation might have been." He accused Interior Minister Hermida of lying in an effort to discredit him.

In a burst of macho prejudice, which at the time he held in common with many Cuban men, he denounced the bisexual

Minister for his "sexual degeneration." After a few days, Fidel's half-sister Lidia broke the news to him that the story was, in fact, true. For Mirta, Fidel's reaction was the final straw. They had already drifted apart personally and she wanted no part in his political activity. Now she began divorce proceedings. When she was granted custody of Fidelito, Fidel raged, "One day I'll be out of here and I'll get my son and honor back, even if the earth is destroyed in the process."

Even though he was in prison he wanted Fidelito away from the influence of the treacherous Díaz-Balarts. He launched a legal suit, and an epic vendetta. "I'm going to do whatever is necessary and I don't care if the suit lasts until the end of time," he said. "If they think they can wear me down and that I'll give up the fight, they're going to find out that I've acquired Asiatic patience. I shall re-enact the Hundred Years War, and I'll win it."

The conditions of his captivity had improved following a visit from the Interior Minister. Hermida told Fidel that he had had no part in putting Mirta on the Ministry payroll. He said no one was questioning Fidel's integrity and honor. Fidel replied that Hermida had, unlike the Díaz-Balarts, acted correctly and his dispute was not with him, but with the dictatorship.

By the end of 1954 that regime seemed stable, but only if you didn't inquire beneath the facade. Cuba resembled a giant Potemkin village. Havana was the Las Vegas of the Caribbean, with nightclubs, bordellos, casinos, skyscrapers and a cast straight out of *Godfather II*. But throughout the island were seething lakes of poverty and smouldering indignation.

Batista, however, felt confident enough to go ahead with promised elections in November, though not so confident as to allow serious opposition. Fidel's supporters used the election period to raise the call for an amnesty for the Moncada prisoners. The two women who had been jailed, Haydée Santamaría and Melba Hernández, were already free and had been fighting to build an amnesty campaign. Among those joining the Amnesty Committee for Political Prisoners were two other young women, Vilma Espín and Celia Sánchez: their lives were to become thoroughly entwined with those of Fidel and his brother Raúl. The charismatic attraction of Fidel was now so great that in the course of the election rallies would be punctuated with cries of "Fidel Castro!"

Some members of the Congress tabled an amnesty bill in March 1955. The government, sure of itself and irritated by the publicity Fidel received from behind bars, said it would agree it if the Moncada veterans renounced insurrection. The prisoners rejected the condition, declaring, "We shall not give up our honor as the price for freedom. We will suffer 1,000 years of imprisonment rather than humiliation." Their intransigence was swiftly vindicated. Complacent and impatient to puncture the mystique gathering around Fidel, Batista signed an unconditional, general political amnesty. On May 15 Fidel and his comrades were released. He greeted his supporters like one of the victorious Spartan warriors, whose history he had absorbed behind bars.

Next page: **Isle of Pines prison, May 15, 1955**
Twenty months after the assault on the Moncada barracks, Fidel and those comrades who survived and were imprisoned were granted an amnesty following a campaign for their release. They returned to political life with their prestige greatly enhanced. To Fidel's immediate right is Juan Almeida, and to his far right his brother Raúl.

chapter 3
Fidel's vision
of Cuba

Viva Fidel! 1955–1959

As we leave the prison... we proclaim that we shall struggle for [our] ideas even at the price of our existence ... Our freedom shall not be feast or rest, but battle and duty for a nation without despotism or misery ...

Fidel composed those words, part of a draft *Manifesto of the People of Cuba from Fidel Castro and the Combatants*, on the steamboat that took him and his comrades from the Isle of Pines to the port of Batabanó. It was his first opportunity in 15 months to collectively discuss with them. The Manifesto was published in the mass-circulation *La Calle* on the morning they arrived in Havana. By then he had well-laid plans to launch the revolutionary 26th of July Movement, taking its name from the date of the Moncada assault.

In so doing, he committed himself to a path that was to see him forced into exile in Mexico, where he imbibed the guerrilla tactics that had been honed on the Republican side during the Spanish Civil War two decades before. It was there that pure serendipity brought him together with a young, wheezy, Argentine doctor—Ernesto "Che" Guevara. The pair, and eighty others, were to return to Cuba in December 1956, crammed aboard a rickety boat called, of all things, the *Granma* (Grandmother). From high up in the inaccessible Sierra Maestra mountain

Previous page: **Sierra Maestra, Oriente province, October 1957**
Fidel contemplates the mountain range where he had been fighting a guerrilla war against Batista's troops for nearly a year. On his sleeve are the insignia for the 26 July Movement, named after the day in 1953 when he led the failed assault on the Moncada Barracks in Santiago de Cuba.

range, with a force that at first could be discounted by the gangsters in Havana, Fidel directed an unlikely guerrilla war that would see the liberation of Cuba within two years.

To observers, that seemed inconceivable in May of 1955 as Fidel stepped out of captivity. He was formally a member of the Ortodoxo party, but the old party system—always sickly—was now in its death throes. Fidel was to remain in Cuba for only nine weeks. He stayed at a small apartment in Havana rented by his sister Lidia. He confided in her, "I must admit that I'm somewhat bohemian and disorderly by nature. Besides there is nothing more pleasant than having a place where a man can throw cigar butts on the floor, without the subconscious fear that the mistress of the house is watching you like a hawk … In the end, there are two things that are incompatible: domestic tranquillity and the busy life of a fighter. It's sensible to keep them as far apart as possible."

But there was, indeed, to be "no feast or rest." A spate of bomb attacks was shaking Havana. Fidel condemned them outright as "inhumane and anti-revolutionary." He asked the question, "Cui bono?"— who benefits? He concluded that the government, which seized on the violence to again clamp down on the opposition, itself had a hand in the attacks. He had said on the day of his release, "No one with any sense can think that setting off a bomb in any old doorway can bring about the downfall of a government." The overthrow of Batista had to come by other means.

On June 12, 1955 Fidel founded the 26th of July Movement. In public he proclaimed loyalty to the Ortodoxo party, calling for "immediate and general elections." But he had given up on the sclerotic chatterers who led the party. He set about drawing to his Movement the brightest, best and most committed elements of the youth—in the Ortodoxo and among the wider radicalized layers of Cuban society, especially the National Revolutionary Movement (MNR).

Danger in Havana

Fidel was the very picture of the charismatic national leader of the anti-dictatorship forces. But the older opposition politicians were in no mood to step aside, issuing words—and only words—that they hoped would erase him from the scene. He sought every avenue to get his voice heard—through newspaper columns, radio and rallies. He rapidly ran up against the tight boundaries of what the regime would allow. He was banned from the airwaves. Students were not allowed to gather to hear him. On June 4 Batista made a speech in which he claimed "the government wants to be patient." Fidel hit back with an article in *La Calle* titled "Murderous Hands!" The paper was closed down, followed a few days later by the closure of *Alerta* after it too published news about him.

Life-threatening danger was closing in on Fidel. Three of his closest comrades formed an armed guard to protect him. He decided not to spend two consecutive nights in the same house. News reached him that the authorities were intending to stage an incident in which he would be killed. The rebels discovered that Fidel's brother Raúl was going to be arrested on false charges. On Fidel's instruction, Raúl sought refuge in the Mexican embassy and then left hastily for exile in Mexico.

Through all this Fidel fought to cohere the new movement around his leadership. There were disputes with those who wanted to steer it towards supporters of the former President Prío. There was jostling for position by those who felt their own roles in the Moncada events were being insufficiently recognized. A few veterans broke with him. A few others came close and then pulled back. He would always remember their indecision.

By now the danger of assassination was paramount; Fidel decided to follow Raúl to Mexico. He left detailed, secret instructions to the leadership of the Movement, the Directorate. Their task was to build revolutionary cells wherever they could across the island. They were to raise funds for the comrades in Mexico, who would raise an armed force which would return by sea to Oriente, where José Martí had come ashore, in the east of the island far from Havana.

There, high in the inaccessible Sierra Maestra, they would begin the guerrilla war that would liberate Cuba. Frank País, appointed head of the movement in Santiago de Cuba, the capital of Oriente, would organize diversionary operations and logistical support once the war was underway. It was a plan of staggering audacity, even insouciance, which might suggest the delusion of failed revolutionary dreamers down the ages … except, that's exactly how it was to be.

Fidel left for Mexico on 7 July 1955. He wrote to his comrade Carlos Franqui, who published the letter in the magazine *Bohemia*:

I am packing for my departure from Cuba, but I have had to borrow money even to pay for my passport … All doors to peaceful political struggle have been closed to me. Like Martí, I think the time has come to seize our rights instead of asking for them, to grab instead of beg for them. Cuban patience has its limits. I will live somewhere in the Caribbean. There is no going back possible on this kind of journey, and if I return, it will be with tyranny beheaded at my feet.

Setting up camp in Mexico

Fidel was yet to turn twenty-nine when he arrived in Mexico City and the sum total of his expeditionary force was himself, his brother Raúl and his old comrade Antonio "Ñico" López. Within days they were joined by a young Argentine, Ernesto Guevara, known to his friends—and later to the world—by the Argentine slang for pal, "Che." They met on 10 July, 1955 at the apartment of María Antonia González, the Cuban wife of a Mexican wrestler. Che had requested the meeting; he had already heard of the young—but seasoned—Cuban revolutionary who had so enraged Batista.

The two took to each other immediately. In his diary, Che wrote, "I met Fidel Castro, the Cuban revolutionary. He is a young, intelligent guy, very sure of himself and extraordinarily audacious. We hit it off well." Che had been in Guatemala the previous year when the CIA engineered a coup to overthrow the popular government of President Arbenz that challenged the stranglehold of the American-owned United Fruit Company over the country. Fidel had experience of this company from his childhood days—it owned the land around his family's farm in Birán. No peasant could bring their crop to market except through United Fruit.

Fidel outlined to Che his vision for a Cuban revolution. They talked all night. Within a few days Che told his soon-to-be wife, the Peruvian activist Hilda Gadea, that he was also to be wedded to Fidel's project. Che, a medical graduate, insisted that he wanted to take part in the expedition not only as a doctor to the group, but as a guerrilla fighter himself.

But who was to forge this small band of dedicated revolutionaries into a skilled fighting force? Fidel sought out the ideal candidate—65-year-old Alberto Bayo.

Bayo, a veteran of the Spanish civil war and an expert in guerrilla tactics, was crucial to training Fidel's fighters. As a commander on the Republican side against the better armed forces of Franco he had argued for the use of guerrilla forces—recalling that the guerrilla fighter had been born in Spain (the word guerrilla means "little war" in Spanish) and had been deployed with devastating consequences against Napoleon in 1808.

He told Fidel, "The man of the guerrilla is invincible when he can rely on the support of the peasants in place." During his sojourn in Mexico, Fidel addressed both terms of the formula: constructing a guerrilla force and ensuring that it would be able to swim in a sea of popular support.

Mexico City was awash with drifters full of half-baked blueprints for revolution. Of meeting Fidel, Bayo later wrote:

Wasn't it amusing? He was asking whether I would commit myself to teach guerrilla tactics to his future soldiers, when he had recruited them and when he had collected the money to feed, dress and equip them, and buy ships and transport them to Cuba. Come on, I thought, this young man wants to move mountains with one hand. But what did it cost me to please him? 'Yes,' I said, 'Yes, Fidel, I promise to instruct these boys the moment it is necessary.'

We would place a man at 200 meters with a hen at his side, using telescopic sights ... We took hundreds, thousands of shots, it was a test of the confidence of our people.

Right: **Mexico City, 1956**
Target practice at the Los Gramitos firing range, where the future expeditionaries prepared for their return to fight in Cuba.

Che and Fidel—a meeting of destiny

Fidel Castro and Ernesto Guevara were to become known to the world simply as Fidel and Che, bracketed together forever, the two giant figures at the peak of the Cuban revolution. Yet it was a partnership that both entered into without a second thought. It was to end only with Che's assassination in Bolivia on October 9, 1967. And not even then. Fidel Castro told me once that even now Che Guevara still appears in his dreams and that in those dreams he and Che are still young men. When the bones of her father were finally repatriated from Bolivia and handed to Che's daughter, she promptly handed them back to Fidel saying that these remains belonged to the people of Cuba.

The two lives had paralleled each other before they met. Both were sons of respectable middle class families; at university both railed against the injustice that characterized the whole of Latin America; both drew on the revolutionary traditions of the continent; and they were of the same generation—Fidel was just two years older. On July 8, 1953, as Fidel prepared for the Moncada assault, Che Guevara was heading off to Bolivia, fired by a similar revolutionary urge "to combat for the liberation of the Americas from United States imperialism."

From Bolivia Che traveled progressively northward to Central America and was in Guatemala in 1954 when the reforming Arbenz government was overthrown in a CIA-choreographed coup. One of Fidel's comrades—Ñico López, who had escaped after the Moncada events—met Che in Guatemala. López assured him that Fidel would be released from prison and might well go to Mexico. From López and other Cuban refugees Che learned more about Moncada and Fidel's movement.

Che considered himself a Marxist. Years after their meeting, Fidel recalled, "He was a Marxist in his thoughts, and a more advanced revolutionary than I was." It was Raúl who introduced the two men. Hilda Gadea, who married Che in Mexico in August 1956, later wrote, "It was stimulating for the spirit to talk with Raúl: he was merry, open, sure of himself, very clear in the exposition of his ideas, with an incredible capacity for analysis and synthesis. This is why he got along so well with Ernesto."

On their first meeting Fidel and Che stayed up all night talking for ten hours. This, I can assure the reader, is a common experience on meeting with Fidel. According to Hilda, Che told her that Fidel was "a great political leader in a new style, modest, who knew where he was going, master of great tenacity and firmness." Che said that Fidel "asked me a lot of questions about the revolution in Guatemala and said how strange it seemed that a medical doctor should work as an itinerant photographer … Within a few hours of our meeting, in the early morning, I had already become one of his future revolutionaries."

Hilda recounted in her book how in the months after meeting Fidel, Che brimmed over with enthusiasm for his planned Cuban revolution. He said that he was:

from the outset, moved by a feeling of romantic, adventurous sympathy, and by the conviction that it would be worth dying on an alien beach for such a pure ideal.

Building an elite force

Alberto Bayo was in exile in Mexico, teaching English and French, and running a small furniture factory. He initially offered Fidel's group three hours of military training a day. Fidel protested, "No, General Bayo, we want from you the entire day. You must give up all your other occupations, and devote yourself fully to our training. Why would you want a furniture factory if inside a short time you will come with us, and we shall be together victorious in Cuba?" He embarked on a long, persuasive entreaty.

Bayo later recalled, "I became intoxicated with his enthusiasm, and he conveyed his optimism to me … Then and there I promised Fidel to resign from my classes here and to sell my business." Over the months, Bayo visited safe houses, rented by Fidel for his trickle of recruits, ostensibly as an English teacher, in fact to give lessons in weapons handling and other military skills.

In an echo of his meticulous preparations for the Moncada assault, Fidel rented a small farm near Chalco as a cover for the group's military training. Bayo sold his factory to a businessman, but he never got the $6,000 he had been promised for it. Fidel gave Bayo $65 a month "to continue the fiction" that he had a stable income. When Bayo's wife discovered the truth three months later, she took on extra teaching duties; Bayo refused to take further money from Fidel, who was worse off than he was, and later wrote books to repay Fidel the $195 he had given the old soldier at the beginning.

In Miami Fidel was briefly reunited with Fidelito; Lidia had taken him out of school to meet his father. The six-year-old Fidelito began playing with cash collected at a fundraising rally. Fidel cried out, "Don't touch it, Fidelito. That money belongs to Cuba!"

Meanwhile, the Cuban regime tried to discredit Fidel by spreading stories that he was misappropriating funds to line his own pockets. The accusations did not dent Fidel's standing in Cuban public opinion, but they struck bitterly at his sense of honor. He hit back with a long missive outlining in detail how had spurned every opportunity to enrich himself. He recalled how he had collected 20,000 pesos to finance the assault on Moncada, and had not spent any on himself. "Yet how many times were we short of milk for my son!" he wrote, "How many times did the hard-hearted electric power company cut off my electricity! … I had no personal income, and practically lived off the charity of my friends. I know what it is like to have a son suffering from hunger, while having in my pockets money belonging to the cause." The money collected in the U.S. was going to buy weapons, set up safe houses and a farm, south east of Mexico City, where serious military training could take place from January 1956. The recruits, swollen in number by arrivals from Cuba, climbed mountains and learnt how to handle rifles.

Political preparations also advanced. Fidel fought to establish contacts with influential Mexicans and Latin American exiles in Mexico City. But his central focus was to shape M-26-7 (the 26th of July Movement) and try to build up sympathy in Cuba. A week after arriving in Mexico he wrote that he was studying the government of General Lazaro Cárdenas, who in the 1930s had expropriated foreign-owned oil companies and instituted far-reaching land reform. Suffering from a bout of the 'flu Fidel managed to finish a draft of a "complete revolutionary program." It became the movement's *Manifesto No. 1 to the People of Cuba.*

Everything I have done up to now and will do has been aimed at preventing, with Cuba's independence, the United States extending its influence over the other countries of the Americas. I have had to work in silence, because there are things which if they were to be publicly known would undermine our victory.

José Martí, last letter, 1895

Left: **Philadelphia, U.S.A., October 23, 1955**
Fidel went to the United States to raise funds to continue the struggle against Batista.

Raising funds for the revolution

The need for funds took Fidel on a speaking tour to the U.S. and, as José Martí had done before, he spoke to gatherings of Cuban exiles and expatriates. He refused to take money from former Cuban government officials who had fallen out with Batista and left with a chunk of the public purse. "Money stolen from the Republic cannot be used to make revolutions," he said. He was prepared to accept money from wealthy Cubans, some of them conservatives, who thought Batista should stand up to the Americans, but their limited aims were not his.

Fidel spoke to an audience of 800 at Palm Garden Hall, New York, and of 1,000 at the Flagler Theater in Miami. There was some skepticism among the anti-Batista émigrés about what this talkative young man would actually achieve. But he came away with $9,000—some of it doubtless from people who were hedging their bets. By the time he returned to Mexico on December 10 his visit had not gone unnoticed by U.S. Intelligence. The FBI opened a file on him and began infiltrating his U.S. support network.

Right: **Cayo Hueso, Florida, U.S.A., December 7, 1955**
Continuing his fund raising, Fidel was always careful not to give the impression that he intended to oppose the interests of U.S. business, and was happy to pose with the flags of both countries. But he knew well, as did the U.S. government, that any challenge to the interests Batista represented would mean just such a challenge—because Batista was an agent for U.S. interests pure and simple.

It makes me sad that I don't have more time for reading. I suffer when I see libraries and lists of books of any kind, regretting that I can't spend my life reading and studying.

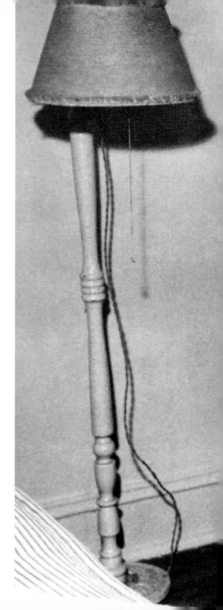

Right: **Miami, December 1955**
Fidel stayed in the house of the revolutionary Felix Elmusa during a stop on his tour following the same fund raising route as José Martí had followed sixty years before.

Fidel under arrest

It was not so much the political pronouncements that Fidel was making, but the seriousness of his preparations to make them a living reality that brought the attention of Batista's regime and the Mexican police bearing down on him. By June 1956 agents were shadowing him. On 21 June Fidel was followed by the Mexican immigration police to a safe house in the Polanco district of the capital. There the police discovered an arms cache. Fidel was arrested. The following day a raid on the training base at the farm outside the city brought more arrests, about forty, and the seizure of much of the group's weapons and supplies. It was another moment of great danger for Fidel and his nascent revolutionary movement. The biggest fear was deportation to Cuba.

But intervention by Mexican friends, including former President Cárdenas, managed to get a judge to order their release. The Interior Ministry relented, but only after a summit of leaders of American states had concluded in Panama: the Mexican government wanted to maintain its reputation as a sanctuary for Latin American exiles. But Fidel's time in Mexico was fast running out. One of those who helped secure his release was the distinguished Cuban writer Teresa Casuso. She was taken to meet Fidel by a young woman who was staying with her, Isabel Custodio. Casuso described the impact Fidel made: "He gave the impression of being noble, sure, deliberate … He gave me a greeting of restrained emotion and a handshake that was warm without being overdone. His voice was quiet, his expression grave, his manner calm and gentle." Fidel stayed at Teresa Casuso's apartment until his release and tried very hard to impress Isabel. Naty Revuelta had already broken off her relationship with him. Fidel had offered to marry her if she joined him in his revolutionary project. She refused. After a while, Fidel proposed to Isabel Custodio and, as was customary at the time, got the permission of her parents. But that engagement lasted only a month. She too shrank back from joining Fidel on the path of sustained armed struggle in Cuba.

Fidel threw himself into recovering from the June raids and rebuilding the movement. He obtained financial support from exiled former Cuban president Carlos Prío, but he had to swim across the Río Grande and make an illegal entry into Texas to get it. The cash enabled Fidel to get his hands on what you might grandiloquently call a "landing craft;" more prosaically, the *Granma* was a barely seaworthy former leisure boat, built 18 years previously to carry a maximum of 25 people!

In October his sisters Emma and Agustina brought Fidelito to see his father in Mexico City for what was ostensibly a two-week trip. Fidel arranged for his son to stay indefinitely with a trusted Mexican couple. But a few weeks later Fidelito was seized while out on a walk by three armed men, who spirited him back to Cuba and the Díaz-Balart family.

With the police and Cuban agents closing in, Fidel accelerated plans for the landing on Cuba. He had, in any case, already imposed a deadline on himself, circulating leaflets saying, "In 1956 we shall return or be martyrs." A police raid on Teresa Casuso's flat on November 21st netted some of Fidel's weapons and precipitated the invasion plan. Fidel sent a telegram to Frank País, the M-26-7 leader in Santiago de Cuba on the east of the island. It said, "The book you ordered is out of print." Decoded, it meant the landing would be near Niquero in Oriente province on November 30th.

The 26th of July Movement, which has conserved intact all its forces and its spirit of struggle, proclaims the need to unite all people, all arms and all resources against a dictatorship that is dividing us, hunting us down and murdering us separately.

Previous page: **Miguel-Schultz Detention Center, Mexico City, 1956**
Fidel (in dark glasses) and many of the group training with him to invade Cuba were held under Mexican immigration laws. Next to him is María Antonia González, at whose house the revolutionaries often met, and where Fidel and Che Guevara (seated, second from left) met for the first time. Juan Almeida is seated center, and Ramiro Valdés is on his left.
Right: **Miguel-Schultz Detention Center, Mexico City, 1956**
Fidel behind bars for the second time.

In Marti's footsteps

We strap on our revolvers, steer towards clearing. Moon comes up red ... we land on a rocky beach.

José Martí

Thus Fidel's hero José Martí recorded in his diary the moment of coming ashore on the beach of Playitas, eastern Cuba, in April 1895. The inspiration for Fidel's landing 61 years later could not be more apparent. Within six weeks of Martí's landing, he was dead. For Fidel death might well have come even sooner.

Fidel and 81 comrades had a nightmarish journey aboard the *Granma* from Mexico to Cuba. They put to sea against high winds and waves, and most of them suffered severe seasickness. The bilge pump stopped working and for a time the heavily overloaded boat had to be bailed by hand. Progress was slower than anticipated. But Fidel had no means of warning members of M-26-7 that his arrival in Oriente province would be delayed by what turned out to be two days. An uprising led by Frank País in Santiago went according to plan on November 30, but by the time Fidel's group landed two days later it had had to be abandoned. Celia Sánchez had got men and vehicles to the planned landing beach ... and waited in vain.

The *Granma* did not find the haven of a beach—rocky or otherwise. It ran aground in a swamp. The 82 rebels had to leave most of their heavy equipment behind as they struggled through the mangrove onto dry land. Moving by night they headed inland, as Martí had done. Ambush by Batista's forces, however, came swiftly.

On December 5 a unit of the Rural Guard caught them by surprise.

There was pandemonium. Fidel fired off volleys from his rifle and roared out commands for an orderly retreat. But it was too late. Fidel and two others were cut off and eventually managed to hide themselves in a sugar cane field. Che was wounded and wandering on his own. Three rebels were killed in the Guards' attack that afternoon; the remaining 79 were dispersed into fully 26 different groups, some of them numbering just one rebel.

Juan Manuel Márquez, the second chief of staff, was quickly captured and murdered. Another 21 suffered the same fate. Twenty-two were imprisoned and 19 others vanished. There were just 16 left from the *Granma* landing, scattered across the lower slopes of the Sierra Maestra.

By the end of the month they had located another three *Granma* survivors. Twenty-three against an army, air force and navy—all sponsored by the U.S. leviathan. Yet within two years the Rebel Army was to enter Havana in triumph.

Struggling to evade capture, Fidel later said, "Our group was completely dispersed. I had two men and two rifles with me." On December 16 the three of them managed to reach the planned rendezvous at the farm belonging to Ramón "Mongo" Pérez, on the western slopes of the Sierra Maestra. Two days later Raúl and four others turned up. On meeting them, the 30-year-old Fidel said, "We'll win this war. We are just beginning to fight." Then Che and his group of eight arrived, among them Camilo Cienfuegos and Juan Almeida. On Christmas day the Rebel Army comprised 16 people— incredibly the key leaders had survived.

Regrouping the rebel forces

To the outside world the rebels had all been reported dead. Fidel's mother, still mourning the death of her husband a few weeks earlier, told the local paper:

I suffer as a mother of soldiers and revolutionaries, but if Fidel and Raúl decide to die, I pray they may die with dignity.

As Batista withdrew his troops and air force, Fidel dispatched Mongo Pérez to tell the MR-26-7 leaders in Santiago de Cuba he was alive and well. They and the movement in Havana reorganized and began to supply the Rebel Army with recruits, money and weapons. Martí's grand strategy had been to draw forces to him and move from the remote east of the island to progressively liberate Cuba from Spanish rule. It was the *leitmotif* for Fidel's campaign, too. It required patience and co-ordination between the Rebel Army and the movement in the *llano,* the lowlands around the cities. Fidel moved eastward, higher into the Sierra Maestra, from where, in January, he launched his first offensive.

The rebels attacked a small military post near the beach at La Plata. Accurate intelligence was vital. Fidel, posing as an army officer, tricked a drunk, local land company overseer, Chico Osorio, to part with the information. During the encounter Osorio boasted to the undercover Fidel that he had killed a rebel and taken his boots. Using the information from Osorio, the rebels surrounded the post at night. When the garrison finally surrendered two were dead, five were wounded and three more were captured. Fidel ordered Che to bandage the soldiers' wounds. He congratulated them for their bravery and let them go. Osorio, however, was executed on Fidel's orders. There is no prettifying guerrilla warfare. The Spanish authorities responded to the war launched by Martí with the creation of the concentration camp—brutally relocating peasants into what the U.S. army in Vietnam would later call strategic hamlets designed to deprive the rebels of support. Batista was to deploy exactly the same counter-guerrilla tactics in Cuba.

That imposed on the rebels the need for an ostentatious display of integrity and honor before both the peasants and those rank and file soldiers who had to carry out orders on pain of death. But it also required developing an equally fearsome reputation for dispensing battlefield justice to those who volunteered themselves for Batista's repressive apparatus. News of the fate of Chico Osorio earned the rebels a lot of goodwill. The overseers were among the men most hated by the peasantry. If this new Rebel Army could stand up to them, then Fidel and his comrades deserved respect.

Fidel understood the lives of the peasants and wanted to show, as Martí had envisioned, that life could be different in the new Cuba he was fighting for. In the areas controlled by the Rebel Army, the peasants were liberated from the daily injustices inflicted by state functionaries. The rebels helped with the coffee harvest high up on the mountain slopes. Instead of seizing food and materials, they paid for them.

While most of the volunteers came from the towns and cities, Fidel was able to build up a large network of support among the peasants of the Sierra Maestra. The hinge for the entire strategy was the relation between this gradually expanding liberated zone in the mountains and the struggle conducted by the movement's militants in the towns and cities.

Our army is tiny, insignificant, compared with the immense and formidable army that we have in the people: men, women, old people and even the children who picture the revolutionaries as heroes out of adventure stories.

Right: **Sierra Maestra, October 1957**
Fidel talking to peasant children outside their house.

Fidel: brilliant organizer and communicator

We had our first successful battle when no one believed we were still alive.

That is how Fidel recalled the attack on the La Plata outpost. Within weeks of the operation the whole world was to know that news of his demise, had, as Mark Twain commented in his famous riposte to reports of his own death, been "greatly exaggerated." Batista moved quickly to crush the embryo of the Rebel Army. An attack by his air force on the rebel camp on January 30 broke up Fidel's forces into three and very nearly finished them off. Their location had been betrayed by Eutimio Guerra, a peasant supporter who had been turned by the army. Guerra guided Batista's aircraft in again on February 7—by now Fidel and Raúl suspected they had a traitor in the ranks.

Fidel refused to be isolated. He established clear lines of communication with the urban leaders of the M-26-7. It was at the first of those regular meetings, on February 16, 1957, that he met Celia Sánchez, a formidable revolutionary who was to play an indispensable role at his side. He was also able to meet up with the leaders of the MR-26-7. There he prioritized the supply of the Rebel Army with recruits and supplies.

Weapons and resources were channeled up to the mountains through the underground conduits of revolutionary cells based in the plains. He turned down suggestions of a second front in the Escambray Mountains in the center of the island as premature. He feared that some of the movement's leaders were emphasizing the gradual strengthening of their own sections at the expense of the Rebel Army.

Such tensions between the two wings of the movement were to recur over the next two years. It was to demand great political skill from Fidel to keep the two in tandem and also to seek allies among the other anti-Batista forces. Some of those allies, and even some of the more anti-Communist elements of MR-26-7 itself, bridled at the influence of Che, a radical Marxist, and at Fidel's dominance.

The movement suffered one of many crises in July 1957. The hugely respected Frank País wrote to Fidel to say that he and Havana leader Armando Hart had decided to revamp the movement in the *llano*, creating more of a federal structure for the National Directorate. He also commissioned a group of intellectuals to work on a program that was "serious, revolutionary and within the realm of possibility." Before tensions burst open between him and Fidel, País was tragically caught and killed by the police in Santiago de Cuba. His fate illustrated the danger faced by the movement in the cities. Thousands defied the police to attend his funeral.

Eight months into the guerrilla campaign, Fidel's movement was establishing a firm base of support. Central to nurturing it was breaking the stranglehold Batista enjoyed over the news media. Fidel embarked on a sophisticated communications strategy to get his message across. Soon, it was not only guns and ammunition that were making their way by mule through the rainforests of the Sierra Maestra; journalists were arriving too, their access alone demonstrating the narrowing compass of Batista's writ. Writers such as Herbert Matthews of the *New York Times* filed reports from the guerrilla camps that shattered the fiction of normality on the island that Batista was desperate to maintain. Meanwhile, a rebel radio transmitter allowed the Cuban masses to hear from Fidel directly and make up their minds about him for themselves.

Interview with Ramiro Valdés

HAVANA 26 MAY 2006

Comandante Ramiro Valdés Menéndez survived the attack on the
Moncada barracks in 1953 and has been close to Fidel ever since. With
Fidel he was imprisoned on the Isle of Pines, was amnestied, left for
Mexico, and returned on the yacht *Granma* to fight in the Sierra
Maestra. He ended the guerrilla campaign as second in command in
Che Guevara's Column 8. After the triumph of the Revolution he
became head of state security and, in 1961, Minister of the Interior.
Since 1996 he has headed Cuba's electronics industry. He is a member
of the Central Committee of the Communist Party and a delegate to the
National Assembly. He is honored as a Hero of the Republic of Cuba.

Comandante, how would you evaluate Fidel as a military commander?

Undoubtedly Fidel is very important in the context of the history of Cuba, and not only in that context. As a military chief in our war of liberation he was able to put the country on the track of sovereignty and independence. In assessing his role you have to take account of not only military but also political factors.

Fidel amassed a great deal of historical knowledge. He was able to make a critical analysis of a wide range of battles in conflicts from the wars of the ancient world through the Spanish Civil War of the 1930s and the Second World War.

He had this tremendous ability to take those events and adapt them to the strategy of liberating Cuba. And without doubt he's a military genius, not only in an immediate theater of operation, but also in the internationalist battles that we have waged abroad. Those battles have been led from here with Fidel, supported by the staff of the Armed Forces headed by Raúl.

Fidel has an amazing capacity for analysis of both political and military events and for anticipating what is going to happen. During the war in Angola, he knew from here in Cuba all the details of the theater of operations as well or even better than our commanders on the ground. He has a great organizational capacity. His is a philosophy of going into details. From that follows the design of the strategy and the tactics, all the way down to where guns should be placed. In our war of liberation, for example, when the enemy columns were marching toward us he knew the optimum moment for an ambush. He knew which man to place where, with which weapon, and which ammunition.

We used 30-06 rifles. The ammunition came from different countries—the Dominican Republic, Mexico and so on. Ammunition from one source could not be used in certain guns. Fidel was checking how many bullets they had, and from what source, and what caliber of weapons. The life of a comrade or the success of an operation could depend on such a detail. It is very rare for something to escape Fidel's attention. One has to acknowledge that he is not an ordinary man. You are always at a disadvantage with Fidel, and this is something that successive American administrations have failed to learn.

Fidel has said that the Moncada attack might have been militarily a mistake. Perhaps it would have been better to go straight into mountains.

On this point, Fidel and I don't agree. But of course, given what I have just said, the one who is wrong must be me! I participated in Moncada and was among those injured. We had expected the soldiers to be sleeping, with their weapons locked away. We would have taken them by surprise if we had not come up against a checkpoint which, according to our reconnaissance, should not have been there. Otherwise, the attack would have been a success. So from the military point of view I don't see it as a mistake, and I don't believe that Fidel does either.

There is also the wider political point of view. We had the alternative of going straight to the mountains. But things would not have been the same without Moncada. The attack made a great impact on national and international public opinion.Fidel and his group became known to the people as a result. The mass mobilization built up pressure to release the Moncada prisoners. It was this that laid the basis for the long campaign in the Sierra Maestra. Moncada also proved that the only person who was able to solve the impasse in Cuba was Fidel.

How decisive was Fidel at the Bay of Pigs invasion?

We were expecting the attack from different places. We had taken measures and reinforced certain areas. We should have had a battalion in the area where they landed, but for whatever reason we had only a platoon. Fidel understood that it was vital not just to throw back the attack but to do so very quickly. Had they succeeded in setting up a beachhead, then a provisional government in waiting was ready to head off from Florida to Cuba. Fidel's knowledge of the area, thanks to his knowledge of the various development projects there, was an advantage. He knew what forces were there, and his personal presence and leadership raised morale. He was, as usual, in the front ranks of the defensive line.

You wouldn't see Tony Blair or George Bush leading the troops in Iraq! Tell me, is Fidel also a good shot?

¡Coño!

You mentioned Fidel's attention to detail and understanding of the terrain. Was this also his style in the international battles the Cuban armed forces were engaged in—for example, in Angola?

Fidel had the image of the terrain in his brain, he didn't even need to look at a map. He could take a geographical element from a map of Angola and describe it as if he had been there. He was the true commander at the battle of Cuito Cuanavale that led to the defeat of apartheid.

It is easy to see that his men adored him and also to see why he has caught the imagination of the youth of Cuba all over the island. Here was an educated, dedicated fanatic, a man of ideals, of courage, and of remarkable qualities of leadership.

Herbert Matthews,

Left: **Sierra Maestra, 1957**
Camilo Cienfuegos (left) and Fidel with some new rebel recruits.

... the most remarkable and romantic figure ... in Cuban history since Jose Martí.

Herbert Matthews

Right: **Sierra Maestra, February 17, 1957**
With Herbert Matthews of the *New York Times,* the first journalist to interview Fidel in the Sierra Maestra.

The peasants began coming to meet us with less fear, while for our part we did not fear their presence, since our forces had increased considerably and we felt more secure against whatever surprise from Batista's army.

Che Guevara

Left: **Sierra Maestra, May 1957**
Raúl Castro is in the foreground and to Fidel's left is Crescencio Pérez, the legendary leader of his peasant network. The photograph was taken by Andrew St. George, a U.S. freelance journalist who most likely also filed reports for U.S. intelligence

151

When I saw the missiles that they aimed at the house of Mario (Sariol), I promised myself that the Americans would pay dearly for what they were doing (in support of Batista). When this war is over, a much longer and greater war will begin for me: the war that I am going to wage against them. I have come to realize that this is going to be my true destiny.

Right: **From *Coronet* magazine, 1958**
A drawing by the magazine's artistic director Rosenzweig, based on a photograph taken by the U.S. freelance journalist Andrew St. George on one of his visits to the Sierra Maestra.

Celia Sánchez: Fidel's right-hand woman

As early as June 1957 Celia Sánchez Manduley had become for Fidel an "essential pillar" of the Cuban revolution. She was to remain so, at his side until her death in 1980. By that time she was a member of the Central Committee of the Communist Party of Cuba and secretary of the Council of State and Council of Ministers. For a quarter of a century she and Fidel maintained an extraordinary bond. She was his gatekeeper and confidante, as well as being an indomitable revolutionary in her own right.

The revolutionary war of 1956 to 1958 saw her emerge as a brilliant organizer and rebel leader. She was born in 1920, the daughter of a doctor from Manzanillo, in eastern Cuba. She grew up knowing the geography of Oriente province very well. As a teenager she climbed the highest mountain there, and in all Cuba, to place a bust of Martí on the summit of Pico Turquino.

That knowledge became indispensable when she became the main conduit for supplies to the rebel army, turning Manzanillo into a staging post for men and arms on their way to the Sierra Maestra. And not just that. "If Fidel wanted a dentist, he wrote to Celia Sánchez. If he wanted to share his enthusiasms, his ambitions, his disappointments, he wrote to Celia Sánchez." Soon Celia moved permanently to the Sierra Maestra.

Left: **Fidel with Celia Sánchez, Sierra Maestra, February 18, 1957**
Fidel is showing Celia how the mechanism of the gun works.

In the Sierra Celia Sánchez became a mother-cum-secretary to Fidel. Several years older than he, she fussed over him, praised him, picked up his cigar butts, cleaned his boots, arranged his meals and his business affairs, and wrote out most of his letters from the scraps of paper he used in composing them. To a visiting reporter Celia was "as serious as a gendarme." As the revolutionary movement grew in size and complexity, she proved to be invaluable to the singularly untidy Fidel and, ultimately, powerful in her own right. Only she had access to a mysterious box that contained the "treasury" of the Rebel Army. Before the end of 1958, as wealthy Cubans paid their "revolutionary taxes," she was said to control more than a million dollars. Those who had dealings with Fidel might resent the influence she wielded over the rebel leader … but they ignored her at their peril.

Celia became the first woman to assume a full military role in the Rebel Army and took part in the attack on El Uvero early on in the campaign. In October 1957 she joined the Rebel Army's general command.

Pedro Alvarez Tabío, director of the Cuban Council of State's Office of Historical Affairs, wrote a touching article in the May 4, 1990 issue of *Bohemia* recalling Celia's contribution during the revolutionary war. She located a house in Manzanillo that could be used to hide men and equipment destined for Fidel in the mountains. It was less than 500 meters from Manzanillo jail. Nevertheless, "upon arriving, Celia realized she had found the place she was looking for to assemble the entire contingent of reinforcements," writes Tabío. "The very proximity to the troops guarding the jail was an additional guarantee. Who would think that the temporary camp for the reinforcements would be set up under the very noses of the enemy? Everything depended on the care taken and the measures adopted to avoid calling attention to themselves.

"This decision was typical of Celia. On that occasion, perhaps more than any other during her activity as a clandestine fighter, she demonstrated fully her qualities for this type of struggle: daring, ingenuity, the ability to mask all suspicious movements, the discipline she demonstrated and that she knew how to instill and demand from all those around her … She was on top of all the details concerning the transfer of combatants and arms; the supply of food, cigarettes, medicine, and items of every type; and attending to the needs of each one of the men assembled there."

Celia had a strong sense of history, which she had developed, like Fidel, in childhood. "Early on she was able to recognize that in addition to the urgent immediate tasks posed by the struggle on a daily basis, it was necessary to devote attention to assembling a documentary testimony of that struggle," writes Tabío. "For example, she preserved detailed balance sheets of expenses from December 1956, during her activities to obtain resources for the survivors of the Granma expedition … From the first months of 1957, the documentary collections preserved by Celia or turned over for safekeeping … began to grow daily. Historians or biographers today can reconstruct in minute detail the truthful story of that heroic and harsh struggle, thanks in large measure to Celia." Her cool-headedness and organizational efficiency also guided Fidel as he set up the post-revolutionary government and moved to consolidate the administration of the new state. She was to remain a central figure in his life until her death in 1980.

Getting the message out

Fidel had asked Faustino Pérez to find a competent foreign journalist who would come to the mountains to conduct an interview and counter the rumor that he had been killed upon landing. The Cuban press was hamstrung by censorship. Pérez's first choice was the American Ruby Hart Phillips, a tough, experienced reporter who would provide an honest account. But he considered her too well known to safely smuggle through the army lines into the Sierra. Phillips suggested instead Herbert Matthews of the *New York Times.* He had spent 40 years on the paper—half of that time as a foreign correspondent covering the Italian invasion of Abyssinia in 1936 and the defeat of the Spanish Republican forces by Franco.

Matthews posed as an American businessman who was looking to buy a sugar plantation. He was driven to Manzanillo and from there was taken by jeep, and then on foot deep into the Sierra. He spent some hours with Fidel and returned the following afternoon with seven pages of notes, which his wife smuggled back to the U.S. A week later, on February 24, the *New York Times* Sunday edition carried the first of three long articles on Fidel and his rebels.

"President Fulgencio Batista has the cream of this army around the area," he wrote, "but the army men are fighting a thus-far losing battle to destroy the most dangerous enemy General Batista has yet faced in a long and adventurous career as a Cuban leader and dictator." He described Fidel's army as "a revolutionary movement that calls itself socialistic. It is also nationalistic, which generally in Latin America means anti-Yankee."

Matthews was clearly impressed with what he saw. He wrote, "Raúl Castro, Fidel's younger brother, slight and pleasant, came into the camp with others of the staff, and a few minutes later Fidel strode in. Taking him, as one would at first, by his physique and personality, this was quite a man—a powerful six-footer, olive-skinned, full-faced, with a straggly beard. He was dressed in an olive-gray fatigue uniform and carried a rifle with a telescopic sight, of which he was very proud …The personality of the man is overpowering. … As the story unfolds of how he had at first gathered the few remnants of the 82 around him, kept the government troops at bay while youths came in from other parts of the Oriente, as General Batista's counter-terrorism aroused them, got arms and supplies and then began a series of raids and counter-attacks of guerrilla warfare, one got the feeling that he was invincible…. Castro is a great talker. His brown eyes flash; his intense face is pushed closer to the listener, and the whispering voice, as in a stage play, lends a vivid sense of drama …"

We have been fighting for 79 days now and are stronger than ever … The soldiers are fighting badly; their morale is low, and ours could not be higher. We are killing many, but when we take prisoners they are never shot. We question them, talk kindly to them, take their arms and equipment, and then set them free … Batista has 3,000 men in the field against us. I will not tell you how many we have for obvious reasons. He works in columns of 200; we in groups of 40, and we are winning. It is a battle against time, and time is on our side.'

The interview was a triumph. Attempts to censor copies of the *New York Times* imported into Cuba were at first self-defeatingly crude (the first issue appeared with holes where the article had been cut out) and then collapsed (visitors from the U.S. brought in copies intact). Radio stations in Florida broadcast excerpts from the interview. Fidel had 3,000 copies of it made and posted to various oppositionists in Cuba. The third installment of the article breached the censors. Then, following the advice of a former CBS executive who advised Batista, the defense minister, Santiago Verdugo, denounced the interview as a fraud—a "chapter in a fantastic novel". The *New York Times* hit back by publishing a photograph of Matthews with Fidel, straining the credibility of the Batista government beyond breaking point.

Perhaps the greatest gain the interview brought Fidel was the projection of his rebellion as youthful, handsome, and idealistic. By the late-1950s the first stirrings of youth revolt against the stultifying conservatism of the post-war years were already apparent in American pop music and Western youth sub-culture, more generally. Matthews captured the spirit of the age exquisitely. After the Cuban revolution brought down the wrath of the U.S. establishment Matthews was to be castigated as a dupe of the "Communist Castro." He was banned by the *New York Times* from covering Cuba. He left the paper, bitterly disillusioned, in 1967 and went to Australia. But in the heady days of 1957 and 1958 he blazed a trail for a succession of Western journalists to make their way to the Sierra Maestra to find out what these young, charismatic, "non-Communist" freedom fighters were up to.

Not all came with honorable intentions. Fidel became particularly suspicious of one visiting American journalist. He said, "He was not asking questions, he was just fooling around, playing a role. I said,

'This is a spy. They've sent us a spy.' But what were we going to do? We couldn't hold a trial and execute him just on suspicion."
After the spy left, Fidel moved camp and repositioned a hut that could be used to identify the base from the air. A few days later aircraft appeared and bombed the hut.

Fidel used the opportunity provided by Matthews' interview to issue another manifesto to the Cuban people. It called for revolutionary action throughout the island. It was part of an ongoing process of communication between Fidel, his followers in the plain, and other anti-Batista forces. His own vision of revolution in Cuba, and his leadership of it, were not uncontested.

José Echeverría, leader of a rival rebel group, had returned to Cuba and had formed an umbrella organization aiming to "strike at the top" of the regime, to proceed through assassination. On March 13 they struck at the presidential palace. They shot their way into Batista's office, but found there only the remains of his lunch and two coffee cups; the dictator had just left by the elevator to his living quarters on the floor above. It was the only way up, and Echeverría's group found themselves unable to reach Batista, even though they were just one floor below him.

The guards rapidly regained control, killing most of the assault force as it tried to flee. Echeverría had seized control of a radio station, but soon found himself surrounded. In any case, the régime had taken the precaution of installing automatic cut-outs on the microphones. He retreated towards the university but was gunned down as his car collided with a police vehicle. The episode underscored the futility of the strategy of assassination. Had Batista actually been killed, there were others in the army command who could take his place. And the failed assassination bid provided the perfect cover for the authorities to clamp down on the opposition.

After seven years of struggle, the democratic victory of the people must be absolute ... The people and the Rebel Army must be more united and more determined than ever, so that the victory that has cost so much blood is not stolen from them.

Left: **Camp at la Plata, Sierra Maestra, October 1958**

La Plata was the rebel army's command base and last line of defense. It had hospitals, electric generators and munition stores, and from here Radio Rebelde broadcast and *El Cubano Libre* was published. Fidel regrouped his troops for the final campaign of the war.

Hail the conquering hero!

A springtime of revolt was sweeping much of Latin America by March 1958. After a decade in power General Marcos Pérez Jiménez had been overthrown in Venezuela. A year earlier the same fate had befallen General Gustavo Rojos Pinilla in Colombia. In Cuba, both Batista and Fidel spoke of an imminent final showdown between the regime and the rebels. In a portent of the vacillation that was to mark the last eight months of his rule, Batista almost simultaneously sought to shore up U.S. and domestic support by offering a degree of liberalization, and also looked to re-equip the army to deal a deathblow to the guerrillas.

Batista announced that there would be new elections in June and lifted some of the most authoritarian aspects of the regime. The liberalization threatened to spiral out of Batista's control. University students clashed with the police. Independent judges began to bring charges against members of the security apparatus. Batista re-imposed authoritarian rule, even though it risked alienating a U.S. Senate that was under pressure for its support for unpopular Cold War dictatorships. On March 20, elections were postponed for five months and Batista took direct control of counter-insurgency operations, announcing he intended to crush the Rebel Army by the end of the summer. That same evening a gathering of American gangsters at the Havana Hilton was told it was too dangerous for them to leave the hotel at night—so that meant it would have been *really* dangerous! And, despite the press censorship, Cuban reporters were beginning to trek into the Sierra Maestra. There, Che had set up a short-wave radio transmitter to broadcast Radio Rebelde, a rebel news service. Throughout much of March broadcasts focused on an impending general strike.

Fidel had discussed the strike with members of the National Directorate of MR-26-7 and had issued a manifesto, *Total War Against Tyranny,* in early March proclaiming that "the strategy of the final blow is based on the general revolutionary strike, to be seconded by military action." The date of April 9 was secretly chosen for the nationwide stoppage. It turned out to be a bitter failure. Fidel called it "the hardest blow suffered by the Revolution during its entire trajectory" adding that "the people had never had as much hope as that day, and we never had so many illusions as we had on that occasion."

Planning for the strike was poor in the extreme. The army had managed to jam most of the rebels' radio transmissions. Crucially, there was lack of co-ordination between the different forces that had any support from the urban working class—it seems that message of fighting unity was not heard by militants in Havana and the other cities. So activists loyal to different organizations approached the strike with an acknowledged sense of disunity.

Batista, however, *had* prepared. The imminence of the strike was an open secret. Fidel was elated when he heard programming on the popular radio station CMQ interrupted on the morning of April 9 by a voice announcing that the strike had begun. "The time has come, Che!" he said. "The time has come! You don't have to wait any longer. You'll be going with us, down to Havana." But the rebel CMQ announcer was quickly taken off air. Batista's forces moved swiftly and ruthlessly to snuff out any sign of an organized stoppage or support actions. Almost everywhere workers were intimidated into work or simply did not know that they were supposed to be part of an insurrectionary strike. In Santiago, workers sustained a significant strike for two days but then, aware of their isolation, returned to work.

It was a terrible lesson in the weaknesses of the movement in the *llano*, the urban underground. Fidel criticized MR-26-7 leaders in the cities for the lack of planning. He wrote to Celia Sánchez, "I must take responsibility for the stupidity of others." The balance within the movement shifted from the *llano* to the Sierra, and within the leadership, decisively towards Fidel. Meanwhile, the Rebel Army had to withstand a major offensive by Batista, emboldened by the failure of the general strike.

The dictator ordered 10,000 men into Oriente province, backed up by heavy artillery and air power. Part of the weaponry had come courtesy of Israel (a sign of things to come for Latin American dictators) via the Somoza dictatorship in Nicaragua. The brutal force was under the command of General Eulogio Cantillo; Batista followed the battle from his base in Camp Columbia, on an Esso road map that had a blank space for the Sierra Maestra. Batista was determined to blank out the voice and image of Fidel, whom he recognized as his nemesis. But the intricate knowledge Fidel had gained of the terrain, and the wellspring of peasant support, were to allow his force of just 300 guerrillas to emerge victorious.

Superior mobility allowed the Rebel Army to move rapidly and gain local superiority even though it was heavily outnumbered overall. When up against a big detachment, Fidel withdrew, setting ambushes in his wake. At the peak of the regular army's advance, Fidel was confined to the central spine of the mountains. But his ammunition supply remained intact. So did his precious radio transmitter. The journalist Ruby Hart Phillips in Havana noted a significant increase in the sale of short-wave receivers.

The campaign lasted 11 weeks, during which Fidel wrote many letters. He constantly called on his forces to conserve ammunition and make every shot count. To enemy officers, he offered the gentlemanly hand of patriotic common interest. "After all," he wrote to General Cantillo, "we are your compatriots, not your enemies … Perhaps when the offensive is over, if we are still alive, I will write to you again to clarify my thinking, and to tell you what I think we, you, and the army can do for the benefit of Cuba." These missives struck at the low morale of Batista's army.

As the rebels began to turn back Batista's advance one incident foreshadowed the even greater battle Fidel was to fight with the force that had helped sustain Batista—the U.S. government. He discovered that bombers, supplied by the U.S. to Cuba supposedly only for external defense, were being refueled at the American base at Guantánamo Bay and that the Cuban air force had just received 300 rockets there. "When I saw the rockets being fired at Mario's house," wrote Fidel to Celia Sánchez, "I swore to myself that the Americans would pay dearly for what they are doing. When this war is over a much wider and bigger war will begin for me: the war that I am going to wage against them. I know that this is my real destiny."

Raúl hit back by kidnapping 49 Americans, 24 of them Marines. There was outrage in the U.S. The kidnapped Americans were released after three weeks, during which the bombing stopped. Weeks later the U.S. confirmed an arms embargo on Cuba. Shamefully, the putrescent British government of Harold Macmillan used the opportunity to supply the Cuban military with 17 Sea Fury planes and 15 tanks. It was something Fidel was not to forget.

By September Batista's army was beginning to fall apart, leaving the way clear for Fidel to go onto the offensive. He had already made contact with the Communist Party, seeing in them a mass organization that could bolster a post-Batista government. He moved his main force into the western plains of Oriente. To the east Raúl's and another column made up the other side of the pincer.

The final push to victory

The cities of Santiago de Cuba and Santa Clara remained in government hands, just. In December, Manuel Urrutia flew in to the Liberated Zone. On Christmas Eve Fidel and Celia Sánchez attended a Castro family dinner in Birán.

President Eisenhower's government overruled the U.S. ambassador to Havana and decided it was in their best interests for Batista to hand over power to a military junta, which would keep Fidel out of power. The man they had in mind was General Cantillo, whom Batista had scapegoated for the failure of the summer offensive. On December 28 Cantillo flew to a meeting with Fidel in Oriente. They spoke for four hours. Fidel said he would not accept a coup or military junta. Cantillo promised his troops in Santiago de Cuba would surrender to Fidel and march with him to Havana. The date and time were set for 3pm on December 31.

On December 30 Che's forces took Santa Clara, the capital of Las Villas. Cantillo persuaded Batista to go. In his letter of resignation he announced that Cantillo "has taken charge" of the new government. Batista flew into exile just after midnight on December 31—something Cantillo had promised Fidel would not be allowed to happen. Fidel was furious at Cantillo's action. It must have seemed like 1898 all over again—a popular rising usurped at the last moment. Through Radio Rebelde he ordered his men to advance: "Revolution, yes! Military coup, no! *Coup d'état* behind the backs of the people, no! *Coup d'état* in agreement with Batista, no! Taking victory away from the people, no!"

The junta in Havana collapsed, barely hours after Cantillo received the congratulations of the U.S. ambassador. The general was placed under house arrest. As news of Batista's fall spread, the streets exploded in joy. A second broadcast by Fidel ordered members of MR-26-7 to maintain order. They emerged from the underground. The following day Che and Camilo Cienfuegos entered Havana. Camilo took control of Camp Columbia, which Colonel Barquín had taken command of the previous day in the name of MR-26-7. Barquín had earlier that year refused to join forces with the Rebel Army. He phoned Fidel's headquarters and said, "Put Fidel Castro on the line." Fidel said, "Tell him I'll speak only to Camilo." As Fidel put it, "Why the hell should I talk to a man who had spurned the Revolution?"

Fidel, now in Santiago de Cuba, received the surrender of the Moncada barracks—surely a delicious moment. He toyed with the idea of declaring Santiago de Cuba the new capital of the Republic. It was to take him five days, and a triumphal march through the country, to get to Havana, by jeep, helicopter, and tank. During those five days he further rallied support and created an exhilarating atmosphere of expectation in the capital, where his men had distinguished themselves by their discipline.

As he stopped in towns and villages, ecstatic crowds came out for him. The *Chicago Tribune* reporter Jules Dubois witnessed the jubilant scenes:

'I must see him! I've got to see him!' one hysterical woman said to me, tears flowing from her eyes. 'He has saved us! He has liberated us from a monster and from gangsters and assassins.'

Fidel entered the capital on January 8—the British ambassador at the time described him as "a mixture of José Martí, Robin Hood, Garibaldi, and Jesus Christ." He spoke from the balcony of the presidential palace and at Camp Columbia, which was thrown open to civilians for the first time. Ruby Hart Phillips of the *New York Times wrote*, "As I watched Castro I realized the magic of his personality … He seemed to weave a hypnotic net over his listeners, making them believe in his own concept of the functions of government and the destiny of Cuba."

He warned of the danger of disunity. He said "some people" had seized weapons from a base. He asked why and against whom they were to be used. The crowd was indignant and demanded the weapons be handed back. Without mentioning the name of the group that had taken the guns, Fidel was able to secure their return without the use of force. Over the decades Fidel was to appeal again and again directly to the people. In the revolutionary year of 1959 it was this extraordinary connection between Fidel, the "Maximum Leader", and the masses in Cuba that was to steer the Revolution through crises and opposition, internal and external.

Left: **Camp Columbia, January 8, 1959**
Surrounded by a human sea, Fidel enters Batista's former military barracks, thrown open to the people for the first time. Just hours before he had entered Havana in triumph and declared: "This is a revolution made by the people and for the people."

I believe in mankind and I believe that new people will emerge, new generations. I have the greatest hope that people more capable than us will arise in the future, better than ourselves.

Left: **With Fidelito in a Havana street, January 8, 1959**
As he entered Havana Fidel caught sight of his half sister Lidia, holding his son Fidelito by the hand. He ordered the tank he was standing on to stop, and took Fidelito in his arms after three years apart.

I believe that if we created an army with twelve men ... which never abandoned a wounded fighter nor struck a prisoner ... then we are the ones who should lead in the affairs of the Republic.

Right: **"Voy bien, Camilo?," Camp Columbia, Havana, January 8, 1959**
After entering the city that afternoon, Fidel delivered a triumphant speech. At one point he turned to Camilo Cienfuegos, who was at his side, and asked: "How am I doing, Camilo?" Camilo replied: "You're doing great, Fidel." At that moment white doves flew onto the podium, one landing on Fidel's shoulder. He took it in his hand, then released it into the air in a gesture that the crowd took as an important omen for the future.

chapter 4
A New Dawn

Building a new Cuba: 1959–1962

At the end of Fidel's speech in Camp Columbia on January 8, 1959, two white doves settled on his shoulder. But the struggle for peace—true peace, which is more than the absence of war—proved a task as Herculean as making the Revolution itself. There was the challenge of constructing a new government in such a way as to preserve the liberal support for the Revolution while beginning the process of radical social and economic reform. Then there was the goal of aiding similar revolutionary upsurges across Latin America. Finally, there was the need to establish relations with other states. And all of this under the shadow of the eagle to the north: interference by the U.S. in Cuban affairs continued with all the old Yankee imperialist arrogance, despite the overthrow of Batista. Indeed, it was soon to embrace economic blockade and assassination attempts, armed invasion and bringing the world to the brink of nuclear war.

Fidel was true to his word in using his undisputed authority to place Manuel Urrutia in the presidential palace. To the post of prime minister came José Miró Cardona, a liberal lawyer who had taught Fidel at university. Only three members of the new government came from the Rebel Army. Just one of them was a member of MR-26-7. Fidel took the title of Military Commander-in-Chief at the head of what were now called the Rebel Armed Forces. He was to be the guarantor of the Revolution, the great communicator.

Previous page: **Havana, November 12, 1959**
Fidel at a television press conference talking about the disappearance of Camilo Cienfuegos in October 1959

The wounds inflicted by Batista on all who had bridled at his rule ran very deep. In many communiqués from the Sierra Maestra Fidel had promised that the cut-throats of the old order would be brought to justice. Batista had been spirited away. If the revolutionary government was even suspected of allowing the same escape for his henchmen, then people would take matters into their own hands. It had happened before after other popular uprisings. Trials deliberated through January and February on the crimes of Batista's war criminals. Fidel wanted to avoid the mobs that attended the fall of the Machado dictatorship in 1933.

The new U.S. ambassador, Philip W. Bonsal, took exception to some of the trials. But even he wrote in his memoirs, "The Castro procedure of setting up special tribunals to try the cases of people who, on the basis of the Nuremburg principles, were accused of serious crimes, could have been an improvement on the earlier method." He noted that "30 years earlier the hirelings of the Machado regime deemed guilty of similar crimes were simply ferreted out by the mob and killed."

CIA chief Allen Dulles, perhaps still not sure what to make of the new government, told a Senate committee: "When you have a revolution, you kill your enemies. There were many instances of cruelty and repression by the Cuban army, and they have the goods on some of those people. Now there will probably be a lot of justice. It will probably go much too far, but they have to go through this."

As it is, Fidel later spoke of around 550 accomplices to Batista's brutality being killed in all—"no child, we have shot no woman, we have shot no old people." The U.S. press called the executions a "blood bath."

Spiheechie Meeko
(Great Warrior Chief)

rank bestowed on Fidel by Creek Chieftain

Right: **Havana, June 16, 1959**
Fidel offers a private dinner to W. A. Raifford, Chief of the White
Birds tribe of the Creek Indians. Raifford honored Fidel for his moral
values and gave him a head dress made from eagle plumes.

I didn't pick up anything more dangerous than a ballpoint pen.

Errol Flynn

Left: **Havana, early 1959**

Errol Flynn, who lived in Havana where he was co-owner of a movie theater in the 1950s, was reportedly a supporter of Batista. But as the political balance shifted towards Fidel, Flynn was contracted by the Hearst Press to write articles about the Revolution, and went on to make a strange and scrappy documentary film favorable to Fidel which only resurfaced in 2001. He then made the last, and probably the worst feature film of his career—*Cuban Rebel Girls*—which was far less sympathetic to Fidel, and left Cuba in a hurry. In the last days of 1958 he made his way to Oriente province in the hope of meeting Fidel in person at the América sugar mill near Santiago de Cuba, on December 27th. But on that occasion Fidel could not make time for Hollywood's fast-fading heart-throb.

It's very difficult to compete against us in any area, not even in baseball do they want to compete with Cuba.

Right: **Havana, 1959**

After the Revolution triumphed, Fidel put together his own baseball team which was named *Los Barbudos*—the bearded ones. They used to play against the top Cuban teams, and matches would often go on into the early hours of the morning, until *Los Barbudos* could hit a home run or otherwise acquit themselves honorably.

It was said that, when the Baltimore Orioles visited Havana in 1999 for the first baseball match between a U.S. professional team and Cuba in forty years, Fidel personally coached the national team. The Orioles won, but only narrowly, and Cuba won the return match in the United States.

In November 1999, when Venezuelan President Hugo Chávez, also a distinguished baseball player, visited Cuba, he and Fidel organized a match between officials of the two countries, in which they both participated. Fidel, who is famous for refusing to accept defeat, brought on a substitute wearing a suspicious looking beard, who turned out to be Cuba's top pitcher.

Restoring a sense of justice

Fidel was enraged by the hypocritical reaction in the U.S. press and Congress to the trials of Batista's war criminals, as they had looked benevolently on Batista's bloody reign. He pointed out that the U.S. supported the dictatorships of Somoza in Nicaragua and Trujillo in the Dominican Republic. The tribunals were short-lived; independent surveys found 93 percent of the Cuban population supported the sentences handed down on the most grotesque figures from the old order. The mass of people had had enough of the fiction of due process and manipulated parliamentary procedure, and the domination of Cuba by U.S. interests, among them the mafia. Fidel told a major rally that counter-revolutionary forces might attempt to assassinate him to derail the Revolution. He proposed his brother Raúl, recognized for his iron discipline and socialist commitment, as his successor in order to demonstrate the futility of such a move.

Fidel's first visit abroad in 1959 was on January 23 to Venezuela, to mark the first anniversary of the overthrow of Pérez Jiménez. He was greeted by huge crowds in Caracas. The president-elect, Romulo Betancourt, said that Fidel would win an election in Venezuela hands down. Fidel called for close co-operation between the two countries. But Betancourt turned down a private request to supply Cuba with oil and a loan of $300 million.

On his return to Cuba, Fidel was forced to recognize that there were two centers of power in the country: one in the presidential palace, the other on the 23rd floor of the Havana Hilton hotel, or at whatever other location the Maximum Leader found himself. There was still goodwill from foreign investors and Cuban businessmen towards the liberal regime of Urrutia. But the transformation of the lives of the mass of the population, promised by Fidel at Moncada and on countless occasions since, had barely begun. Tensions between Fidel and the more conservative elements of the new government were apparent. On February 13th Prime Minister Cardona resigned. He had, as most Cubans wanted, moved against the mafia-run bordellos and casinos. But he had not put in place any alternative employment or retraining for the thousands of Cubans who worked in them. Fidel was besieged by waiters, croupiers, and others who feared for their livelihoods. He argued to slow the process and ensure there were new jobs created instead of lengthening already long unemployment lines. Cardona resented the intervention. Fidel was appointed to replace him on February 16, telling reporters, "We do not intend to leave things as they are." Now the government moved in a progressively radical direction.

In March price controls were introduced over electricity and telephones, which had an immediate impact on improving the standard of living of large numbers of Cubans. A minimum wage for sugar cane cutters and limits on the price of medicines came next. In May, came the centerpiece—agrarian reform.

At a mass gathering of peasants in the Sierra Maestra Fidel reprised his commitment from Moncada to cap landholdings and redistribute estates to the peasants. Landowners would be allowed 1,000 acres; anything above that was to be expropriated, though some of the big plantations and cattle holdings were exempted as they depended so much on economies of scale. The nationalized land, 40 percent of that under cultivation, was to be broken into plots of 67 acres. The larger plantations were to be run as co-operatives. "From now on," said Fidel, "the children of the peasants will have schools, sports facilities and medical attention, and the peasants will count for the first time as an essential element of the nation." The first land to be nationalized belonged to the Castro family in Birán.

The Cuban Revolution established, from the first day, that it would always respect the will of the peasants and that no peasant would ever be pressured to join their land with that of another so as to create larger holdings.

Left: **Cuban countryside, 1960**

A peasant showing his property title, acquired as a result of the Agrarian Reform Law.

Dealing with vested interests

Five U.S. sugar producers, which had their hands on two million acres, were given generous compensation to be paid over 20 years. But the government calculated the value on the basis of their tax returns. Years of tax avoidance were to come home to roost leading to brazenly hypocritical opposition to land reform by the plantation owners, backed by the U.S. government. "That was the first law," said Fidel, "which really established the break between the Revolution and the country's richest, most privileged sectors and with the U.S. and the transnational corporations." Fidel himself headed the National Agrarian Reform Institute (INRA), which from May oversaw implementation of the land redistribution.

The economic reforms brought a fall in unemployment, a rise in living standards and a consumer boom. But they also antagonized the vested interests in Cuba and posed sharply the need to industrialize the country if economic development were to be sustained. Both these factors were expressions of the fundamental dilemma—how to navigate opposition from the U.S. and the Cuban elite, and how to find allies who could assist the creation of a new society. Fidel moved carefully, but refused to attenuate the social and economic program to the interests of big capital.

In October, he dramatically responded to attempts by liberal capitalist elements in the government to contain the reform program. He appointed Che Guevara as Governor of the National Bank. The popular story at the time was that Fidel asked a group of trusted comrades who among them was an economist. Che raised his hand, believing Fidel had asked who was a communist.

In the weeks following the Revolution Fidel had turned to the Communist Party to provide a counter-weight to the liberal establishment forces in the government. He had to proceed cautiously in order not to provide an excuse for the U.S. to intervene directly. Fidel met the leadership of the Communist Party at various locations outside Havana. Blas Roca, the party's general secretary, recalled Fidel saying, "Shit, we are in government now, and yet we still have to meet illegally!"

In April of 1959, Fidel visited the U.S. at the invitation of the Society of Newspaper Editors. He wanted to use the trip to dispel negative publicity about the Revolution and to narrow the scope for any campaign to overthrow the new government. He hoped to establish aid and trade relations. But he insisted that the Cuban delegation should not open the subject. "The Americans will be surprised," he said, "We will be in a better bargaining position." He found himself having to fend off reporters' questions about the trials of Batista's henchmen. But on the streets he found a very warm welcome. A handful of pickets outside the Cuban embassy had to admit they had been hired by anti-Fidel Cuban businessmen.

He tailored his speech to the themes of national independence, and invoked the New Deal recovery program of depression-hit 1930s America. Even the notion of national sovereignty caused tension. On meeting a State Department official who was "in charge of Cuban affairs", Fidel retorted, "I'm the only person in charge of Cuban affairs." His speeches to newspaper editors and students were well received. He offered friendship with the U.S. and even maintenance of the mutual defense treaty. If a breach was to come, it would be the U.S. government that would initiate it. He met Vice-President Richard Nixon, who, it was later established, had enjoyed the hospitality of the mafia in Havana. Nixon was disturbed by Fidel's "almost slavish subservience to the prevailing majority opinion" of the Cuban people and found him "incredibly naïve" about the spread of Communism.

[He is] ... either incredibly naive about communism or under communist discipline.

former Vice-President Richard Nixon
commenting on Fidel Castro

Right: **White House, Washington, D.C., April 1959**
Fidel visited the United States at the invitation of the Society of Newspaper Editors. He had requested a meeting with President Eisenhower, but was told that the President was away for the week "playing golf," and instead could only meet with Vice-President Richard Nixon.

The forces of opposition

The U.S. State Department's confidential assessment of Fidel's visit was more prescient than Vice-President Nixon's. It feared Fidel would not alter the "essentially radical course of his revolution … It would be a serious mistake to underestimate this man." After the U.S. he visited Canada and then Argentina for an economics meeting of representatives of the Organization of American States. There he proposed the U.S. launch a Marshall-style aid package of $30 billion to stimulate growth across the continent. But he withdrew his proposal when it became clear that other representatives would not embarrass the U.S. government by voting for the scheme. While Fidel had gone out of his way to assuage U.S. opinion during his visit, the incompatibility of the reform program in Cuba and the interests of big business was fast becoming apparent. Those who wanted to hold back the reforms began to jump ship.

In June, the commander of the air force, Díaz Lanz, left for the U.S., denouncing the influence of Raúl and Communist activists in the restructured armed forces. He voiced his true opinion when he told a U.S. Senate committee that events in Cuba were an internal matter for the U.S. With Lanz went Frank Sturgis, chief of security. The two of them would return on a bombing raid, one of a huge number of attacks and acts of sabotage that were to be unleashed on Cuba during the early years of the Revolution. A young woman who had caught Fidel's eye, Marita Lorenz, went over to the CIA and returned to Cuba to steal documents from his office.

President Urrutia denounced Lanz's defection, yet lent it credence by himself condemning the left turn in the Revolution. On July 17 Fidel announced through the pages of *Revolucion* that he was resigning as prime minister, citing Urrutia's obstruction of radical reform as the reason. His television address shocked the nation. Huge protests engulfed the island. Crowds gathered outside the presidential palace demanding Urrutia's resignation. Fidel had gone directly to the people, and they had thundered their answer.

Urrutia resigned, replaced by Osvaldo Dorticós, who was to remain president for the next 17 years. Fidel spoke to a crowd of half a million in the Plaza Cívica. They roared their approval for 10 minutes. He agreed to stay on as prime minister. The peasants who had traveled to Havana waved their machetes in the air and pledged to defend the Revolution from its enemies. Not for the last time he had taken an apparent defeat—a high profile defection—and galvanized the people into deepening the Revolution. But the enemies of the Revolution—within and without—had only just begun their campaign of destabilization.

A senior figure in the Rebel Armed Forces, Huber Matos, resigned after Raúl was appointed Minister of the Armed Forces. His departure took the gloss off a 2,000-strong congress of tourist agents Fidel had convened in Havana to secure foreign income. The congress was further interrupted when a B-26 bomber flew over Havana piloted by Díaz Lanz. It dropped leaflets, and explosions were heard across the city. Two people were killed and 50 wounded. It was one of many incidents that forced the government to take action to defend the Revolution. At this point tragedy struck. Camilo Cienfuegos, one of the great leaders of the Rebel Army, was killed when his light aircraft went missing on a flight to Havana.

Next page: **Havana, 1959**
Fidel signing the Nationalization Law with Cuban President Osvaldo Dorticós looking on.

CIA plots to overthrow Fidel

It was not until March 17, 1960 that President Eisenhower signed an order for covert action to overthrow Fidel. Operations by the CIA, the mafia, and right wing Cuban groups were already well underway. Fidel had received many warnings of assassination plots and had to go everywhere with bodyguards. There were bomb attacks on factories and cane fields set ablaze in a campaign of sabotage. The dictator of the Dominican Republic, General Trujillo, made contact with anti-Fidel conspirators who had taken to the mountains of central Cuba. Two of Fidel's comandantes convinced them they had come over to the plot. They sent a fake message to Trujillo, who sent a planeload of weapons and a second carrying nine Batista supporters, who went to what they thought was a safe house. Fidel himself walked through the door and carried out the arrests.

The safety of Fidel and the Revolution depended on the people. That required organizing a national militia. And that meant arms. U.S. pressure closed down the sale of weapons from the West. The Tory government in Britain refused to replace the aging 17 Sea Fury planes it had sold to Batista. Fidel responded, "If we cannot buy aircraft, we shall fight on the land, if the time comes when we have to fight. If they don't sell us aircraft in England, we shall buy them from anyone willing to sell to us." That meant turning to the Soviet Union.

In October 1959 Fidel began a series of meetings with Alexander Alexeyev, the head of the Soviet Tass news agency in Havana. Fidel suggested hosting a Soviet trade fair in Havana. He argued against an exchange of embassies first as it might play into the hands of the U.S. In February 1960 Soviet Deputy Prime Minister Anastas Mikoyan visited Havana and signed a deal agreeing to import 425,000 tons of sugar that year and a million tons in each of the next four. Payment would be mainly in oil, fertilizers, industrial goods and technical expertise. It was a lifeline against the threat of U.S. economic blockade, which was soon a grim reality. Deliveries began in the spring. U.S.-owned oil refineries, under pressure from Washington, refused to process the Soviet crude. Fidel took over the refineries and brought in Soviet technicians. The U.S. government cancelled sugar imports. Fidel in turn nationalized U.S. assets in Cuba. The time during which Fidel had bought relative freedom from U.S. aggression was now at an end.

In March 1960, a French ship, *La Coubre*, blew up in Havana harbor, killing 81 people and injuring hundreds more. Fidel suspected U.S. sabotage and said so, raising the slogan, "Homeland or Death, We Shall Prevail!" The Technical Services Division of the CIA looked at various plots against Fidel that could have been dreamt up by "Q" in a James Bond movie: exploding cigars and a powder that would make his beard fall out. There were several, serious attempts to put poison pills in Fidel's food.

Soviet premier Nikita Khrushchev announced that the Monroe doctrine of undisputed U.S. hegemony in the Americas was dead, adding, "The only thing to do with something dead is to bury it, so that it does not poison the atmosphere." The Organization of American States, at the behest of the U.S., issued the San José Declaration condemning the intervention of "totalitarian states" in the region. Fidel hit back with the Havana Declaration calling on the Latin American people to break with imperialism. Tensions were growing when Fidel flew to New York to attend the General Assembly of the United Nations in September 1960. On the way, he asked his chief of security if they had a Cuban escort plane. When told the answer was no, Fidel said, "What a mistake! If I were running the CIA, I'd shoot down the aircraft at sea and report it as an accident." A nervous journey ensued.

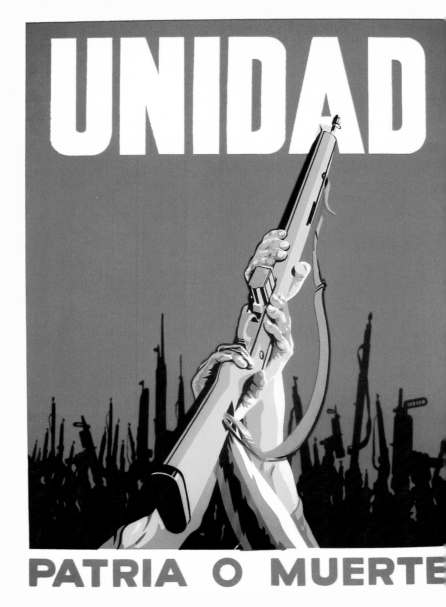

UNIDAD

PATRIA O MUERTE

Without culture
a people cannot
be free.

José Martí

Left: **Poster based on a contemporary photograph**
The poster's title "Unity—Fatherland or Death" took up José Martí's call to arms from the 1895–98 independence war. Fidel was later to adapt it to "Socialism or Death."

Speaking to the world: Fidel at the UN

In New York, Fidel was aggrieved that the Shelburne Hotel refused to put up the Cuban diplomatic delegation without a cash advance. The Shining Prince of the black liberation movement, Malcolm X, took them to the modest Theresa Hotel in the run-down, black neighborhood of Harlem. The poet Nicolás Guillén, thought a plaque should be erected on it, with the inscription: "Fidel Castro took shelter here on the dramatic night of September 19, when, pursued by the injustice and stupidity of the Eisenhower administration, he found generous asylum with the black people of New York City."

Fidel met many journalists and radical activists at the hotel. I once asked him what he made of Malcolm X. "He was a great man, Malcolm," he replied, "but he was a little ... dangerous." And Fidel's abiding memory of the visit was: "The day Malcolm arranged a picnic for all of us in Central Park ... The Cuban leadership and Malcolm's Muslim brothers all stretched out in the heart of New York City. I was terrified the water bottles would get mixed up and our Cuban rum would find its way down the throats of Malcolm's non-drinking bretheren!" He met Khrushchev there, too—the two leaders pointing out to assembled journalists the grotesque racial and class inequality that scarred America. Khrushchev told journalists he was a Fidelista, though he didn't know whether Fidel was a Communist. Jawaharlal Nehru of India and Gamal Abdel Nasser of Egypt also made their way to 125th Street.

At the U.N. building itself, Eisenhower pointedly refused to invite the Cubans to a lunch reception for Latin American delegates. Fidel told reporters, "We are not sad. We are going to take it easy. We wish them a good appetite. I will be honored to lunch with the poor, humble people of Harlem. I belong to the poor humble people." He hosted a steak dinner for a dozen black hotel staff from Harlem. The left wing poets Langston Hughes and Allan Ginsberg joined sociologist C Wright Mills and other members of the Fair Play for Cuba Committee at a sponsored reception at the Theresa Hotel.

The General Assembly meeting saw a clash between the U.S. and the Soviet Union, and also marked the entry onto the world stage of several non-aligned states, newly liberated from colonialism. Fidel's address to the U.N. assembly was four and a half hours long. He left two days later aboard a Soviet Il-18: the U.S. authorities had impounded the two Cubana aircraft the Cuban delegation had arrived in as a payment for debts a Miami advertising firm claimed it was owed by Havana. As he boarded, Fidel said in hesitant English: "The Soviets are our friends. Here you took our planes—the authorities robbed our planes. Soviets gave us plane." The aggressive behavior of the U.S. and the attempted Cuban alliance with the Soviet Union were to characterize future relations.

The U.S. went way beyond impounding planes. In October Eisenhower's government began what was to become a total economic embargo on Cuba. The following January his Democrat successor, John F Kennedy, signed off on a secret plan drawn up by the outgoing administration to launch an armed invasion of Cuba cobbled together from the detritus of the Batista years. The Bay of Pigs débâcle in April 1961 set the U.S. on an obsessive course of confrontation with Fidel and the Cuban people.

Previous page: **Cuban countryside, February 1960**
Fidel accompanied Soviet Foreign Minister Anastas Mikoyan on a tour throughout Cuba.

I don't know
if Fidel is
a communist;
what I do know
is that I'm a
Fidelista!

**Nikita Khruschev,
former Soviet leader**

Left: **Theresa Hotel, Harlem, New York, September 20, 1960**
Fidel meets Soviet Prime Minister Nikita Khruschev for the first time during his visit to the XV General Assembly of the United Nations.

Fellow delegates, I take the opportunity to tell you that there are many mothers in the fields of Cuba and in this country who are still waiting for a telegram of condolence for the assassination of their sons by U.S. bombs.

Right: **Theresa Hotel, Harlem, New York, September 1960**
Fidel meeting with Indian Prime Minister Jawaharlal Nehru. On the left of the photograph is the Cuban Foreign Minister Raúl Roa.

I believe there is an original sin in the approach to the Middle East conflict—the attempt to impose peace unilaterally and exclude the international community.

Left: **Entrance to Theresa Hotel, Harlem, New York, September 1960**

With Gamal Abdel Nasser, President of the United Arab Republic. Fidel and Nasser united with leaders such as Nehru of India and Tito of Yugoslavia to promote a revolution without frontiers which was to become the Non-Aligned Movement.

He was a great man, Malcolm, but he was a little ... dangerous.

Left: **Theresa Hotel, Harlem, New York, September 1960**
When the Cuban delegation was thrown out of its Manhattan hotel it was black leader Malcolm X who arranged for them to stay in Harlem.

Ernest Hemingway: support for the revolution

Fidel is a great admirer of Cuba's famous resident, the writer Ernest Hemingway, who lived in Havana. Hemingway kept out of Cuba's internal politics but had well defined views on the Revolution itself. He and Fidel met only once—at the award ceremony for the annual Ernest Hemingway Fishing Tournament in 1960, at Havana's Barlovento Yacht Club. Hemingway presented Fidel with the prize for catching the biggest blue marlin. The author had expressed his deep regard for Cuba in August 1956 when he donated the Nobel prize he had won for *The Old Man of the Sea* to the the church of the famous virgin known as the *Caridad del Cobre* on a mountain overlooking Santiago de Cuba. It has an extraordinary sanctuary with many treasures. One of the most unusual of these is the gold religious medal that Fidel's mother Lina presented to protect him in the Sierra Maestra.

I believe completely in the historical necessity of the Cuban revolution. I do not mix in Cuban politics but I take a long view of this revolution and the day by day and the personalities do not interest me ...

Ernest Hemingway

Left: **The five-peso Cuban coin minted in honor of Ernest Hemingway** Hemingway won the Nobel prize for Literature for his novel *The Old Man of the Sea,* which was set in Cuba and whose heroic protagonist is modeled on the Cuban fisherman Gregorio Fuentes.

Yo no digo cree, sino lee. Leer es crecer.

I don't say believe, but read. To read is to grow.

Literacy campaign slogan

Left: **Sierra Maestra, 1961**

Peasants learning to read and write. Young volunteers from the cities fanned out across the countryside to wage the most successful campaign against illiteracy ever, which lasted through the year 1961. Cuban literacy teachers are today continuing that campaign throughout the countries of Latin America.

Interview with Abel Prieto
HAVANA 25 MAY 2006

Abel Prieto is Cuba's Minister of Culture. He previously held the posts of director of the publishing house Letras Cubanas and president of the Union of Cuban Writers and Artists. He is a painter and an internationally translated novelist.

You are from a younger generation…

Not so young. I have a grandson … I was born in 1950. I was eight when the revolution happened. My father was a member of the 26th July Movement. Later he became Vice-Minister of Education, working with Armando Hart, and I grew up hearing a lot about Fidel, including before the Revolution. He was a very important symbol for my family.

Do you remember when you first met him?

I remember meeting him personally and him having a strong impact on me at the end of the 1970s. It was at a meeting of intellectuals, one of the Casa de las Américas award ceremonies. He was someone whom I was used to seeing on television, and at various public events, but with too many people between him and me. I remember that Gabriel García Márquez was there, and Armando Hart, the Minister of Culture at the time. And a group of young writers, including myself. He had a tremendous magnetic attraction, a special ability to create a special ambiance around him. I became President of the Cuban Writers and Artists Union in 1988 and began working with Fidel directly. Then I experienced a different impact. I discovered a person with a far-sighted, strategic vision who at the same time is concerned with the smallest details. A very unusual mixture. He has a close relationship with culture.

José Martí said that culture is the only weapon the people have. Has Fidel always seen culture in the same way? Is he a cultured man?

I think he has an enormous culture. He has a very impressive sense of history. If Fidel talks to you about the 19th century battles against Spain it is as though he is reliving them. He analyzes whether the battle could have been won if a different decision had been made. He has a strong literary culture too. He's very familiar with the great 19th century novels of Victor Hugo, Tolstoy, Dostoevsky and Balzac. I don't think he is so very keen when it comes to poetry, but he has read the most important Spanish poets. But when it comes to narratives, he practically devours them, especially historical books. He relates very easily with people from the cultural sector. It was very beautiful what Fidel said yesterday when you were with him, about how he celebrated his 70th birthday in the house of a poet. He has a strong interest in the plastic arts and feels very comfortable among musicians and painters. He has no prejudices when it comes to culture. Martí said that culture is more important for a people than its industry, the spiritual culture in its widest sense. I remember a meeting of the Union of Cuban Writers and Artists in 1993. I was president of this organization at the time. It was during the depths of the crisis we called the Special Period—there were blackouts, shortages of essentials, the calorie consumption of the people had fallen very low, there was no fuel for transport. The U.S. was trying to strangle us with its blockade. And what Fidel said at that meeting was that the first thing we must salvage is culture. He saw culture as essential for the defense of our national identity, and for the defense of the best of universal values. His conception of culture is not chauvinistic. The first book that was published after the Revolution, when the national printing house was established in 1960 under the direction of the famous Cuban writer Alejo Carpentier, was not a Marxist textbook or some speech by Lenin … t was Don Quixote de la Mancha. A book that Fidel loves very much. The most important novel of all time. It was printed on newspaper presses, which had been nationalized by the Revolution. An edition of 100,000 copies was printed on newsprint. A crazy number at that time. A very beautiful craziness. Including the engravings by Gustave Doré. There were four volumes in all, costing just 25 cents for the complete set, one peso at the time. They were sold on the newspaper stands, alongside the regular newspapers. This is very instructive—Fidel never sees things just on a local level.

There is one exception that I mind about—he didn't like the Beatles.

Well, I am fanatical about the Beatles! When we unveiled a statue to John Lennon, twenty years after his murder, on December 8th, 2000, Fidel made an incredible statement. Here in Cuba the Beatles' music had not been played on the radio, it had been distributed underground. Not even original records, pirate ones. I remember in 1967 when the first Beatles song was played on the radio, in fact I wrote a story about it. But during the inauguration in the year 2000 Fidel said that he had never been aware that the Beatles had been prohibited. And you can be sure that if Fidel had been part of a decision to ban the Beatles he would have explained exactly why. This made me very happy. Here I was with Lennon and with Fidel, two figures that I admire greatly—a friend of mine says that I am a Marxist-Lennonist! We made a political mistake. Minor officials had taken the decision to play on the radio mediocre Spanish rock—including atrocious Spanish versions of the Beatles—but not the real thing. I imagine it was because they associated English as the language of the enemy.

Was there a photograph of Fidel with John Lennon's statue?
Nearby, yes, but he didn't wanted to be photographed sitting next to John Lennon because he thought too much would be made of it.

One last question. If there had been no Fidel Castro, what would Cuba be today? Would there have been a Cuban revolution?

I think there would have been a revolution. But at certain key moments of the Revolution, I don't know how we would have resisted. This is very difficult to know, but for instance with the collapse of the Soviet Union … in the year 1990…it is possible that without Fidel the Revolution might have collapsed. This is my own personal opinion. The role of Fidel during the worst moments of the crisis was absolutely decisive. There may have been earlier crises when, without Fidel, the Revolution might have collapsed. His leadership at times of great danger has been decisive, and especially in the war against the Americans. Fidel understands intimately how the Americans will react in any situation. Here in the 1950s there was a revolutionary situation. The Batista *coup d'état,* the terrible corruption of the political classes, the fact that we were essentially an American colony … But Fidel put his seal on events. Fidel's obsession with education, with public health, with equality, his internationalism…has meant that this small country in Latin America could contribute to the fall of apartheid in South Africa. We recently sent 1,500 doctors to help earthquake victims in Pakistan.

The Bay of Pigs invasion

Fidel declared that 1961 was to be the "Year of Education." An ambitious program of literacy and other classes was to serve both as a centerpiece of the social gains the Revolution would bring and also as a direct economic response to the first stage, announced by the U.S. in October 1960, of what would become a total embargo. The Year of Education did make it into the history books and, more importantly, into the lives of millions of Cubans. But the year 1961 became better known for the attempt by right wing Cuban forces, in close alliance with the U.S. government, to overthrow Fidel through invasion. In most of the world the events of April that year are known as the Bay of Pigs invasion; in Cuba, they refer to them as Playa Girón.

The youngest president in U.S. history, John F. Kennedy, took office, emerging victorious from a tight race against Republican Vice-President Richard Nixon. Hostility to Fidel and the Cuban revolution had featured strongly in the closing weeks of the campaign. While Kennedy was keen to offer a break from the conservative Eisenhower years, he had no intention of being "soft" on Communism, Cuba, or Castro.

So it was John F. Kennedy who simultaneously authored the Alliance for Progress, a program of Latin American land reform that Fidel had foreshadowed months into the Revolution, and also signed off on the plan to invade Cuba that the Eisenhower administration had dreamt up. The CIA was charged with forging a single front from the right wing, anti-Fidel forces in Miami—the political equivalent of scooping up mercury with your hands. Young men were taken to training camps in Guatemala, a bulwark of pro-U.S. influence following the 1954 coup. The would-be invasion force was called Brigade 2506, the name taken from the identity tag of one of the recruits who was killed in training. Many of the officers were former members of Batista's army. Meanwhile in Cuba, the CIA stepped up aid to armed anti-Fidel groups. Such was the scale of destabilization that Fidel complained in January that 80 percent of the staff at the U.S. embassy were spies! The number of hit-and-run attacks on Cuba's shores increased. CIA director Allen Dulles was confident it was only a matter of months before Fidel was ousted.

But, through an impressive array of informants, Fidel knew about the base in Guatemala, though the CIA managed to keep the details of the planned invasion secret—including from the Cuban invaders. Fidel divided his army and militia into three zones in the east, center, and west of the island. He expected a diversionary attack at one end with the main assault elsewhere.

In early 1961 Brigade 2506 was transported from Guatemala to the Caribbean coast of Nicaragua. It numbered about 1,400 men in five battalions of infantry and one of paratroopers, supported by artillery and five tanks. Nicaraguan dictator General Somoza—reportedly referred to by President Roosevelt as a "sonofabitch … but OUR sonofabitch"—came to wish the invasion force well, asking them to present him with some hairs from Fidel's beard.

On April 13 the Brigade set sail in seven ships, with the U.S. navy providing a thinly veiled escort. Some of the ships had been lent to the CIA by the United Fruit Company, which Allen Dulles was embroiled in and in whose interest the Guatemalan coup had been organized. At the same time another ship steamed from Florida to launch a feinting attack on the east of the island, much as Fidel had anticipated. He was informed of the suspicious ship off Guantánamo Bay late on Friday, April 14th.

The invasion force lands in Cuba

From his military post Fidel ordered 12 militia battalions in Oriente to move to the coast, ensuring the diversionary landing did not take place. In the early hours of the following day, eight U.S.-supplied B-26 bombers painted with the emblems of the Cuban Air Force took off from a base in Nicaragua. Six of them bombed and strafed three Cuban airfields, one pulled out through engine trouble and the last flew straight to Miami with carefully placed bullet holes to support the fiction that the planes had defected from Cuba. The attack damaged runways and destroyed several aircraft. Seven men were killed and 52 wounded. But, in what was to prove a costly failure for the invasion, some targets were decoys. A few Cuban planes managed to fly and all four of Fidel's airworthy Sea Furies remained intact.

Despite a cacophony of claims from Miami about defections Fidel was rapidly able to confirm that no Cuban pilots were missing. He appeared on television to scotch talk of defections and to describe the attack as "twice as treacherous as Pearl Harbor and a thousand times more cowardly." At the funerals of those killed in the raids, which took place the following day, Sunday, Fidel declared, "What the imperialists cannot forgive us is that we have a made a socialist revolution under their noses." It was the first time he had described the Revolution as socialist. He had planned to make that a part of his May Day speech but, in a typical gesture, he responded to the attack on Cuba by accentuating the most radical aspects of the Revolution.

A few hours later, at around 1 A.M, the invasion force reached the southern coast of Cuba without being detected. Landing craft began ferrying troops to the beaches in the Bay of Pigs, a narrow inlet stretching deep into the Zapata peninsula. Coral reefs slowed them down, but there was little armed resistance in the sparsely inhabited area. The landing zone was a strip of dry land beyond which lay the Cienaga de Zapata swamp. This was so remote that a small militia outpost took over an hour to get to a radio telephone to raise the alarm. Fidel was informed that troops were landing at the Playa Larga in the Bay of Pigs and at Playa Girón ten miles further east. Paratroopers had also reportedly been dropped to take control of the three roads that passed through the swamp. He phoned a trusted officer, Captain José Ramón Fernández, commander of the militia officers school south of Havana and ordered him to take charge of the militia units near the landing site. Fidel ordered an attack on the beachhead without delay. He did not want to give the invaders time to consolidate, militarily or politically: he feared that they would establish a provisional government, which the U.S. would recognize and use as a pretext for overt intervention. He urged on the people: "Forward Cubans! Answer with steel and with fire the barbarians who despise us and want to make us return to slavery."

Fidel swiftly set about organizing what remained of the air force—just eight serviceable planes. At 4.30 A.M. he phoned the air base and spoke to the senior pilot, Enrique Carreras, who was strapped into his Sea Fury. "Lad," he said, "you've got to destroy those ships for me." At dawn two Sea Furies and one bomber sighted two ships in the Bay of Pigs and on the second run were able to damage both. The freighter *Houston* still had one of its two battalions on board when it was hit. It ran aground. Some men were drowned and a lot of equipment was lost. The other ship, the *Barbara J* contained CIA "advisers," who were running the command post, and had to retreat when it was hit. After refueling, the Sea Furies delivered a second strike causing a huge explosion on the freighter *Río Escondido*. It went down with a lot of food, ammunition and what would prove to be vital aviation fuel. The remaining ships retreated.

I captured I don't know how many prisoners, and I saved the life of one that same night, who asked: 'Kill me!'

Right: **Play Girón (Bay of Pigs) invasion, April, 1961**
Fidel jumping from a Soviet SU-100 tank during the battle against
the Cuban émigré mercenary invaders.

Fidel takes direct command

The invasion force was supported by 15 B-26 bombers. But they took three hours to reach Cuba from Central America, meaning they were in the air over the Bay of Pigs for just 40 minutes. The plan was to use an airstrip near the village of Girón, but loss of aviation fuel meant it was never operational. The air battle revealed Cuban ingenuity against superior forces. The Cuban Air Force had skillfully equipped three T-33 training planes with machine guns. They proved very effective against the slow B-26s and were able to shoot down four. Four of the aircrew killed were members of the Alabama Air National Guard, proving U.S. involvement. At a presidential inquiry a month after the Bay of Pigs invasion, Air Chief of Staff, General Thomas White, testified, "Well, I really believe the Cuban Air Force had a whale of an effect on the bad outcome ... I was surprised to find that [the T-33s] were armed."

By 8 A.M. Captain Fernández had assembled two battalions of militia at the Australia sugar mill on the northern edge of the swamp. Fidel ordered him to advance and take the village of Palpite, through which ran a new road. On hearing that the village had been occupied without resistance, Fidel ordered a further advance. The militias engaged the invasion force's second battalion. But they had to advance on a very narrow front, with swamp to both sides of them. The resulting casualties were very heavy. But the operation had a big psychological impact. The invading forces had convinced themselves that the Cuban militia would not put up a fight and, in fact, were simply waiting to go over to the "liberators." Fernández's charge shattered that illusion.

Fidel decided to take direct command. He drove from Havana at hair-raising speed, reached the Australia mill in three hours and set up headquarters there. Troops and militia from Cienfuegos engaged the invading battalions that had landed at Playa Girón. Artillery arrived to bombard the forward positions. A small consignment of tanks supplied by the Soviet Union also joined the battle—their crews had to learn how to operate them on the way there! But the invasion force also had effective tanks. The hard fighting edged towards a standstill.

Meanwhile, Celia Sánchez was at the Havana command post informing Fidel of wider developments. Communications on the battlefield were rudimentary, with Fidel issuing written orders for dispatch to different units. But he had one major advantage. With every hour that passed he was able to reinforce his position and receive continuous supplies. The invasion force, by contrast, was cut off. Not for the last time an internal uprising that the CIA had predicted in support of the invasion proved a mirage. As for more overt U.S. action—such as the deployment of its own aircraft— Kennedy feared a major escalation with the Soviet Union. Raúl was in New York rallying support for Cuba at the United Nations.

After two days of fighting, the commander of Brigade 2506, Pepe San Román, radioed the CIA to say the only remaining option was evacuation. The voice that came back should stay in the minds of all who might consider playing the U.S. stooge. "Sorry Pepe," it said, "You've done everything you could. You've fought well. Break off and scatter. Good luck. Don't call me again." Three days after the landing 1,189 of the invasion force had surrendered and about 110 were dead. Fidel had lost about 180 troops and militia. It was a stunning victory by a small country against a superpower and it reverberated around the world. Fidel made sure of that.

It was very difficult to counter-attack because there were only two roads crossing ten kilometers of swamps. That made those two roads a kind of Pass of Thermopylae.

Left: **Playa Girón (Bay of Pigs) invasion, April, 1961**
Fidel directing operations from his tank.

Exposing U.S. complicity

Fidel took journalists to see the battlefield and on April 20 spent four hours on television demonstrating with maps, charts, and captured CIA documents how the victory had been won and how complicit the U.S. had been in the invasion. On April 26 he went to the Sports Palace to interrogate prisoners, who were taken aback that they were treated well and not executed as their leaders had told them would happen. In an exchange with one prisoner, Fidel said wryly, "This gentleman is the first prisoner in the world who gets a chance to debate with the leader of a nation he came to invade."

Fidel wanted to return the prisoners to the U.S. but, in recognition of the damage inflicted by the invasion, sabotage attacks and the embargo, he called for five hundred bulldozers in return. The negotiations continued for the next 18 months before, in December 1962, the U.S. finally agreed to exchange $53 million of food and medicine for the prisoners. A week later Kennedy flew to Miami to watch Louisiana State beat Colorado in the Orange Bowl. He spoke to surviving members of the invasion force and promised their standard would one day fly in a "free Havana." But Havana was already free and at Playa Girón a huge billboard had been erected, saying, "Giron—the first imperialist defeat in the Americas."

Playa Girón was a humiliating disaster for the U.S. state and its right wing Cuban allies. To the same extent, it hugely boosted Fidel's standing in Latin America and across the globe. In an interview two months after the failed invasion, Fidel said, "Their problem was that they did not have a guerrilla mentality, like we do, and they acted like a conventional army. We used guerrilla tactics to infiltrate their lines, while attacking steadily from the air and on the ground. You must never let the enemy sleep."

A quarter of a century later Fidel reflected, with great magnanimity, on why Kennedy had gone along with the scheme:

Kennedy had inherited the whole plan of Girón from the Eisenhower government. At that time, Kennedy was, from my point of view, unquestionably a man full of idealism, of purpose, of youth, of enthusiasm. I don't think he was an unscrupulous man. I don't have that concept of Kennedy. He was, simply, very new, you might say—besides, very inexperienced in politics although very intelligent, very wise, very well prepared, with magnificent personal qualities. I can speak of experience and inexperience in politics because when we compare ourselves now with what we knew then about politics—the experience we had in 1959, 1960 and 1961—we are really ashamed of our ignorance at that time. Twenty five years have elapsed, and Kennedy only had a few months in the government.

The U.S. establishment's reaction to the Bay of Pigs came quickly in the conclusion of the Taylor board of inquiry, handed to Kennedy in mid-June. "There can be no long-term living with Castro as a neighbor," it said. The following month, at his speech marking the anniversary of the July 26th assault on Moncada, Fidel said, "This is a life-or-death struggle that can only end with the death and destruction of the Revolution or of the counter-revolution." Renewed confrontation the following year gave a terrible immediacy to prophesies of "destruction."

¡Mercenarios por compota!

Give us baby food and you can have your mercenaries back!

Slogan at Cuban marches at the time

Right: **Washington, D.C., April 1961**

A group of Cuban émigré mercenaries met with Eleanor Roosevelt to negotiate with the U.S. government for the release of the 1,200 mercenaries taken prisoner in Cuba. The negotiations dragged on for eighteen months, until the U.S.A. agreed to send $2 million in cash and $50 million of baby food to Cuba in exchange for the prisoners. The Cubans declared, correctly, that the Bay of Pigs was "the first defeat of U.S. imperialism in the Americas."

America's calculated aggression

We want to live in peace … I want to say to Americans: do not be deceived by the propaganda of our enemies. Keep in mind the efforts we are making for the prosperity and happiness of our country. Let us be friends.

Fidel made this overture in an interview with *Look* magazine as early as 1959; in fact he took every opportunity to make gestures of friendly relations with Cuba's northern neighbor. But, as he had told Celia Sánchez in the Sierra Maestra, he knew the Revolution he was leading would bring him into conflict with U.S. interests throughout the hemisphere. That has led to repeated charges of subterfuge by the American right.

Fidel was very candid in his visit to the U.S. in April 1959. He said Cuba was setting out a new course, fiercely independent from the U.S. and invoking the most radical democratic traditions in the Americas. Subterfuge came from the U.S. establishment as it became apparent it could not tolerate the implementation in Cuba of principles it purportedly stood for.

The U.S. recognized the Urrutia government on January 7, 1959. Three days later U.S. Ambassador Smith, a friend of Batista's, resigned. He was replaced by Philip Bonsal, an experienced diplomat who spoke fluent Spanish and whose father had been a war correspondent in Cuba in 1898.

Fidel described him as "friendly, cordial and knowledgeable about Cuba—a good ambassador" following their first meeting in March. Yet five days later the U.S. National Security Council was already discussing Fidel's assassination and how to undermine the

Revolution. The CIA station chief in Venezuela had been alarmed at Fidel's visit: "It seemed to me that something like a chain reaction was occurring all over Latin America after Castro came to power. I saw…that a new and powerful force was at work in the hemisphere."

In October President Eisenhower ordered the CIA to fund counter-revolutionary Cuban groups. Fidel, bear in mind, had offered generous compensation to U.S. companies in Cuba and had enacted a land reform program that the U.S. itself had foreshadowed with its agrarian policy in occupied Japan at the end of the Second World War.

By December the head of the CIA's Western hemisphere division was writing a memo to his superiors, including Richard Bissell, who had been responsible for the coup against the Arbenz government in Guatemala in 1954. It said:

Many informed people believe that the disappearance of Fidel would greatly accelerate the fall of the present government

In January 1960, Roy Rubottom, Assistant-Secretary for Inter-American Affairs, told the National Security Council how policy had evolved:

"In June [1959] we had reached the decision that it was not possible to achieve our objectives with Castro in power … In July and August we had been busy drawing up a program to replace Castro. However, some U.S. companies reported to us during this time that they were making some progress in negotiations, a factor that caused us to slow the implementation of our program. The hope expressed by these companies did not materialize. October was a period of clarification."

Plans for an invasion of Cuba, supported by an internal campaign of destabilization, were discussed at a top level CIA meeting in March 1960. "Unless Fidel and Raúl Castro and Che Guevara could be eliminated in one package … this operation [would] be a long drawn out affair," said one of the participants. The scale of the sabotage campaign was revealed in a secret CIA memo the month after the Bay of Pigs invasion in April 1961.

Some "800 sabotage operations destroyed 300,000 tons of sugarcane in the period prior to the invasion; another 150 arson attacks devastated 42 tobacco warehouses, two paper factories, a number of shops and 21 apartments belonging to Communists; and bombs were set off at a power station and the railway station." Eisenhower gave strict orders that the U.S. should officially appear to have nothing to do with all this.

In August 1960 the CIA established contact with the mafia to unleash an assassination plot, one of many. FBI director J. Edgar Hoover wrote a memorandum identifying the role of mafia boss Salvatore "Momo" Giancana in October that year:

"During recent conversation with several friends, Giancana stated that Fidel Castro was to be done away with very shortly … He allegedly indicated that he had already met with the assassin-to-be on three occasions … Giancana claimed that everything had been perfected for the killing of Castro, and that the 'assassin' had arranged with a girl … to drop a 'pill' in some drink or food of Castro's."

The girl was Marita Lorenz. She couldn't find it in herself to place the poison, later saying, "Love proved stronger." Other attempts on Fidel's life included a barman who was to place pills of botulism poison in his milkshake and a planned bazooka attack while Fidel attended a boxing match.

These repeated assassination efforts, the campaign of violence and sabotage, and the threat of invasion, which culminated in the Bay of Pigs, are the backdrop for the security measures undertaken by Fidel and the Cuban government. These included surveillance of counter-revolutionary groups, establishing an efficient intelligence network and mobilizing a national militia. Amid all the cant from anti-Castro organizations in the U.S. there is never any recognition that the security apparatus in Cuba is a direct consequence of American attempts to overthrow the government and assassinate Fidel, attempts which began within weeks of the Revolution, when it was overwhelmingly acclaimed among Cubans. Fidel responded to each wave of U.S. aggression by deepening the social content and popular base of the Revolution. Commenting three decades after the Revolution, he said:

"We were carrying out our program little by little. All these aggressions accelerated the revolutionary process. Were they the cause? No, this would be an error. I do not pretend that the aggressions are the cause of socialism in Cuba. This is false. In Cuba we were going to construct socialism in the most orderly possible manner, within a reasonable period of time, with the least amount of trauma and problems, but the aggressions of imperialism accelerated the revolutionary process."

U.S. hostility to the Cuban revolution predated Fidel's turn to the Soviet Union for assistance. It was, and is, rooted as much in the inability of the U.S. state to tolerate popular, independent leaders in the Americas as it is in the domestic and foreign policies Fidel has implemented.

The Cuban Missile Crisis

With U.S. hostility to Cuba undiminished following the Bay of Pigs, Fidel moved more explicitly toward the Soviet Union. Soon, the island of Cuba and its six million people were in the maw of the Cold War confrontation.

In December 1961 Fidel declared: "I believe absolutely in Marxism … Did I understand it at the time of Moncada as I understand it today after 10 years of struggle? No. Did I have prejudices about Communism? Yes. Was I influenced by the propaganda of imperialism and reaction against Communism? Yes. Did I think Communists were thieves? No, never. I always thought Communists were honorable, decent people." And the following month he explicitly endorsed the doctrine of the Soviet state: "I am a Marxist-Leninist and shall be a Marxist-Leninist until the day I die."

The response from the Soviet leadership in the first few months of 1962 was cautious. A Cuba that was part of the socialist family of nations was an explicit challenge to the U.S. and drew the Soviet Union directly into the defense of the island. Khrushchev, who had described himself as a *Fidelista* when the two leaders met in New York, warned fellow Soviet leaders that Fidel was "a young horse that hasn't yet been broken. He's very spirited. He needs some training. We'll have to be careful." They preferred to see Fidel describe Cuba as "progressive," putting it in the same category as Ben Bella's Algeria or Nasser's Egypt, rather than an outright socialist state.

Nevertheless, Fidel pressed on in speeches and in deeds. In what he later described as a mistake, he even adopted aspects of puritan Soviet public morality with negative consequences for the culture of personal liberation that had erupted in the two years since the fall of Batista. Still the Soviets were wary of being seen to antagonize the U.S. Fidel's Second Declaration of Havana called for Latin America to rise up against its northern overlord. "You cannot imagine the tremendous reprimand we received from the Soviets," said Fidel many years later, "They were totally opposed to our support for the revolutionary movement … the only thing we got from the Soviet Union was worries."

By the spring Fidel was perturbed that his overtures to the Soviet Union were not being fully reciprocated. There were also mounting economic problems as the U.S. embargo bit deeper. And, there was that bane of post-revolutionary societies: creeping bureaucracy. He spoke out against inefficiency and what Lenin had once called the mentality of the "committeemen."

By that time, opinion had shifted in the Soviet leadership toward a more active engagement with Cuba and a more assertive policy toward the U.S. in the western hemisphere. The Politbureau agreed a plan to station medium range nuclear missiles on Cuba. Soviet leader Nikita Khrushchev outlined the logic: since the October revolution the Soviet Union had been surrounded by hostile forces. The U.S. had missiles stationed on the borders of the USSR. Wasn't it time the U.S. felt what it was like to be threatened in that way? Fidel later outlined the thinking of the Cuban leadership:

"We did not like the missiles. If it was a matter of our defense alone, we would not have accepted the missiles here. But do not think it was because of the dangers that would come from having the missiles here, but rather because of the way in which this could damage the image of the Revolution in Latin America … I thought: if we expected the Soviets to fight for our cause, to take risks for us, and if they were even prepared to go to war for our sake, it would have been immoral and cowardly not to allow the presence of the missiles here."

Fidel's case: self-defense for Cuba

For Fidel the prestige of the stirring revolution in Latin America was at stake, and, a matter of honor, standing by an ally. Work began on the missile sites. Raúl went to Moscow to discuss the deployment. Che went in August to tie up loose ends. The stationing of missiles was handled with the greatest of secrecy. Fidel warned the Soviets that this would lose them the moral high ground in the ensuing confrontation with the U.S. He was right. American U-2 spy planes constantly overflew Cuba at high altitude. In September a worried President Kennedy called up 150,000 reservists. On October 16 he was handed photographs proving that not only surface-to-air batteries but medium range nuclear missiles were being installed. The U.S. Chiefs of Staff unanimously agreed to a massive air raid.

Events now moved at a ferocious pace as the world held its breath. Fidel called up nearly half a million men and women to repel any attempted invasion. On Monday, October 22 Kennedy imposed a quarantine around the island, deploying the U.S. navy to intercept and turn back any Soviet ship on its way to Cuba.

Fidel responded with his own address that same evening: "What have we done? We have defended ourselves. That is all. Were the imperialists expecting that after their first hostile act, our people would surrender, the Revolution would raise the white flag?" The following day he spelled out how the standoff went to the heart of what the Cuban revolution represented:

"All these events are really the culmination of a policy pursued by the United States—not the United States, but the imperialists, the warmongers, the most reactionary circles of the United States— against our country since the triumph of the Revolution … Our progress, our independence, and our sovereignty were always undercut by the policy of the Yankee government, this is, intervention for imperialist ends ... All their attempts failed. U.S. governments are accustomed to solving the problems of Latin America by very simple means: above all, by *coups d'état* carried out by reactionary military cliques controlled by their embassies... the interventions in our continent are well known—the intervention in Haiti, in Santo Domingo, in Nicaragua, in Mexico—from which they wrested the part richest in minerals and oil ... Things occurred exactly this way up until the triumph of the Cuban Revolution."

He ridiculed the idea that Cuba was aggressive to the U.S. Its posture was defensive, but it refused to go the way of the Congo, which had been invaded under the pretext of U.N. support for international law:

We can clearly state that all the countries can rest easy, every country in Latin America, every country of America—the United States—because we shall never be the aggressors. We shall never be the ones to take the offensive. But in the same way we declare this clearly and honestly, we also declare that neither shall we be easy victims of any aggression. And we also declare, with the same determination and the same certainty, that we will know how to defend ourselves and we will repel any aggressor. That is what our weapons are for....We reject definitively any attempt at monitoring, any attempt at inspection of our country. Our country will not be inspected by anyone.

(Zorin) made the mistake of ignoring the real debate, which should have been about the sovereignty of Cuba, its right to defend itself.

Right: **U.N. Security Council, New York, October 25, 1962**
On the right Soviet Deputy Foreign Minister Valerian Zorin denied the evidence from aerial photographs of Soviet missiles in Cuba that U.S. Ambassador Adlai Stevenson presented to the United Nations.

Khrushchev's secret deal

Our people have unfurled a banner of justice. Our people have freed themselves of vice, depravity, exploitation, and the moral and material poverty of the past. And our people are convinced of what they are doing. This is the historic role they are playing, convinced of the prestige they enjoy, of the faith that other peoples of the world have placed in them. And because they are convinced of this, they are able to look ahead calmly. All of us, men and women, young and old, are united together in this hour of danger. And our fate, the fate of all revolutionaries and patriots, will be shared by all of us together. And victory, too, will be shared by all of us together! Patria o muerte! Venceremos!

The day after Fidel made this declaration, October 24, U.N. Secretary General Sithu U Thant appealed to the Soviets to accept inspections in the interests of world peace. Tensions escalated, but behind the scenes and unknown to Fidel, Khrushchev was looking for a compromise. On October 27 a Soviet SAM shot down a U-2 over Cuba. The U.S. Air Force wanted an immediate and massive bombardment. But the next day a deal was done: Khrushchev agreed not to station the missiles; secretly the U.S. said it would withdraw its own from Turkey. On the evening of Sunday, October 28 Celia Sánchez took the call with news of the deal. Next to her, Fidel exploded into an epic rage. Quite simply, he had not been consulted. The deal said nothing about the U.S. ending its embargo of Cuba and it even required the Cubans to accept low-level U.S. reconnaissance flights. Fidel told the visiting U.N. Secretary General that he rejected the deal and would not allow inspections or overflights. He later said:

"I am certain that if the low-level flights had been resumed, we would have shot down one, two or three of these planes … I was at the San Antonio air base … I went there and waited for the planes. I knew there would be a counter-strike if we fired, and possibly we would have many casualties. I thought it was my duty to be there, in a place that would be attacked, but the planes did not come that day." The Soviets sent Deputy Prime Minister Mikoyan to plead for Fidel to back down. The day before his arrival Fidel said:

"We have not violated anyone's rights. We have not attacked anyone. All our actions have been based on international law. We are the victims of an embargo, which is an illegal act, and of an attack by another country … The United States has repeatedly violated our air space. This business of inspections is just another attempt to humiliate our country. Therefore, we will not accept it."

Fidel kept the Soviet Deputy Prime Minister waiting, and waiting. In the end, the issue was resolved by the Soviets agreeing over Fidel's head to withdraw their bombers from Cuba and accepting aerial inspection at sea to prove that the missile sites had been dismantled and shipped out. The U.S. embargo around Cuba stayed. Fidel felt bitterly let down by the Soviet leaders' performance.

¡Nikita, marikita,
Lo que se dan, no
se quitan!

Khrushchev, you
little poof, what
you give you don't
take back!

A popular chant on Cuba's
streets at the time of the
Missile Crisis

Right: **Havana street, October
1962**
The Cuban people prepared for
the possible destruction of their
country.

chapter 5

A place in the world for Cuba

On the world stage: 1963–1970

The 1960s were to thrust Cuba even more prominently onto the international stage. For Fidel the central strategic dilemma, which the Missile Crisis had laid bare in October 1962, was how to secure friendly relations with the Soviet Union and at least neutralize U.S. aggression while at the same time attempting to seed the process of revolution across the Third World.

Fidel sensed acutely the isolation of Cuba in the wake of the missile crisis. The U.S., while not completely recovering the ground lost at the Bay of Pigs, certainly felt emboldened after the Soviet withdrawal. Fidel spent some days back in the Sierra Maestra, from which he had emerged victorious almost three years earlier. Cuban public opinion castigated the Soviet handling of the crisis. For Fidel, if the Soviets were not going to be reliable allies, how was he to defend and industrialize Cuba? Then he received an unexpected letter from Khrushchev. He recalled:

On January 31 1963 ... Khrushchev wrote me a lengthy letter, really a wonderful letter. It is 31 pages long ... a beautiful, elegant, friendly, very friendly letter. Some of its paragraphs are almost poetic. It invites me to visit the Soviet Union ... Tempers had been cooling down by then; they had been quite hot. I accepted the trip.

He intended to stay a few days; he ended up staying nearly six weeks. He was 35. Both he and the Cuban Revolution were young, but tempered beyond their years.

Previous page: **Havana, 1970**
Fidel at the house of his brother Raúl and Vilma Espín, president of the
Federation of Cuban Women.
Above: **Moscow, May 1963**
Khruschev greets Fidel on his post-Missile Crisis visit to the Soviet Union.

Welcome to the USSR!

The Soviet Union had never seen anything like the six week visit by Fidel in the spring of 1963. Still smarting from the Soviets' poor performance during the Missile Crisis, he was nevertheless determined to heal relations. There were many firsts in the 40 days he spent there. He visited 14 cities, made dozens of speeches and was fêted wherever he went.

He was made a Hero of the Soviet Union, and received the Order of Lenin and the Gold Star—a clutch of honors never previously handed out to a foreigner. Khrushchev promised that Soviet engineers would design and build a combine for harvesting Cuban sugar. Fidel said he would adopt Soviet methods of organizing work and production.

But still he wanted answers over why the Soviets had backed down without apparent gain during the Missile Crisis. Years afterwards he recalled:

I put a lot of questions to all the Politburo members I met. I asked one of them, 'Tell me, how was that decision made? What were the arguments used?' I couldn't get a single word out of them. They wouldn't answer the question. Of course, you can't be impertinent and say, 'Listen, answer me!' For all my questions, I couldn't get an answer.

At a relaxed meeting at Khrushchev's dacha, the Soviet leader did inadvertently mention Italy and Turkey, from where the U.S. had withdrawn its missiles in the aftermath of the crisis. Fidel promptly intervened.

I said, 'Nikita, would you please read that part again about the missiles in Turkey and Italy?' He laughed that mischievous laugh of his. He laughed, but that was it. I could see that he was not going to repeat it. As the saying goes, you don't talk about nooses in the house of a man who has been hanged.

Fidel uttered nothing but praise for all things Soviet on his return to Havana. The U.S. government responded with a more aggressive policy of covert operations. Fidel had attempted through back channels to explore less confrontational relations with the Kennedy administration. It was not only the renewed warmth between Havana and Moscow that put paid to that.

There was the pathological opposition of sections of the U.S. establishment to what the Cuban revolution meant in the Yankee hemisphere. Fidel, while publicly extolling the Soviets, who were at the time preaching "peaceful co-existence" between the capitalist and socialist camps, remained determined to inspire revolutionary developments across Latin America and beyond. He authorized Che to publish a treatise on guerrilla warfare. It was to become a reference point for countless young radicals by the end of the decade and was seen as a tilt toward Mao's China.

Next page: **Nikita Khruschev's country dacha, Soviet Union, May 1963**
Seated in foreground, from left to right: Leonid Brezhnev—who the following year was to succeed Khrushchev as First Secretary of the Communist Party of the Soviet Union—Fidel, Khrushchev and Captain Emilio Aragonés.

The fight for survival

Fidel had to navigate international tensions while taking to the front ranks to secure Cuba's economic future. The flight of skilled engineers, combined with sabotage, encouraged by the U.S. and right wing émigrés, was devastating the economy. Cuba's dependence on sugar as its predominant export crop had long been identified by nationalists with the country's domination by U.S. business interests. But the early hopes of the Revolution that the economy could be rapidly diversified and industrialized came up against the grim reality of the U.S. embargo.

How was Cuba to develop while cut off from its traditional trading partner 90 miles to the north? Fidel set about transforming agriculture so that sugar—which made up 80 percent of Cuba's exports—could be the means to accessing industrial goods and oil from the USSR. The mammoth scale of the task became apparent when Hurricane Flora ripped through Cuba in 1963. Fidel personally directed rescue operations and his presence at one farm after another spurred on the workers to make up for the losses.

It was against this backdrop of a fight for economic survival that Fidel brought in military service and a drive to strengthen discipline throughout production.

Previous page: **Soviet Union, May 1963**
Photographs taken during Fidel's six week visit to the Soviet Union.
Right: **Cuban poster, in Soviet social realism style**
The slogan reads: "Be ready for war."

Death of a President: November 22, 1963

The event that became synonymous with the phrase, "Where were you when…?" found Jean Daniel, the foreign editor of the French magazine *L'Express,* interviewing Fidel in Havana. He recorded his response to the news of the assassination of President John F Kennedy.

Fidel had previously heaped scorn on Kennedy, comparing him with the pirate Henry Morgan. But he was now telling Daniel that he felt that Kennedy was showing signs of flexibility. Then he took a call from President Dorticós. Turning to Daniel he said, "It's bad news." As Kennedy's death was confirmed on the radio he said:

I'll tell you one thing—at least Kennedy was an enemy that we had got used to. This is a serious matter, an extremely serious matter.

When the U.S. radio reporter started talking about Jackie Kennedy's bloodstained stockings Fidel was horrified: "What sort of mind is this? … There is a difference in our civilizations after all. Are you like this in Europe? For us Latin Americans, death is a sacred matter." News emerged that the assassin, Lee Harvey Oswald, had claimed to be a member of the Fair Play for Cuba Committee. Fidel promptly went on air to explain that Cuba had had nothing to do with the assassination. He suggested that it would be more likely the work of those who wanted a more aggressive policy against the island than Kennedy's.

And a more belligerent policy is exactly what emerged under President Johnson. It left Fidel even more reliant on Khrushchev. A tentative rapprochement between Cuba and the U.S. was already taking place behind the scenes when John F. Kennedy was assassinated. No observer would have guessed so from the tone of Fidel's speeches. In September 1963 he was telling reporters that Kennedy was the "Batista of his time", a "cretin" from an "oligarchic family." But that same month William Attwood, who had written about the Cuban Revolution for *Look* magazine, conveyed to the U.S. government a conversation he had had with the Guinean ambassador to Havana.

It suggested Fidel was prepared to make "substantial concessions" to improve relations with the Americans. The U.S. State Department's assessment was that "we have something to gain and nothing to lose." Attwood was authorized to meet the Cuban ambassador to the UN.

The following month, another possible line of contact opened up. Daniel was in Washington on his way to Cuba to interview Fidel. Attwood secured a meeting between him and President Kennedy. The President said no country had suffered more from "economic colonialism, humiliation and exploitation" than Cuba—and at the hands of the U.S.

He remained very cautious about Fidel, but wondered whether he had mellowed since the Missile Crisis. He told the journalist: "You can tell me when you come back."

In Havana, Daniel found arranging a meeting with Fidel far more difficult than with Kennedy in Washington. He spent three weeks seeking an audience. On November 19 he was about to leave empty handed, but his flight was delayed. He retired to his hotel, where without announcement Fidel walked through the front door and proceeded to spend from 10 P.M. to 4 A.M. the following morning answering questions.

According to Daniel, Fidel devoured with "passionate interest" reports of what Kennedy had said at the Washington meeting the month before. Fidel said he thought Kennedy was sincere, but:

I have not forgotten the Machiavellian tactics and the equivocation, the attempts at invasion, the pressures, the blackmail, the organization of a counter-revolution, the blockade, and, above everything, all the retaliatory measures that were imposed before—long before—there was the pretext and excuse of communism.

He said Cubans simply wanted to be "accepted as we are! We are socialists. The United States is a capitalist nation. The Latin American countries will choose what they want." He said he believed Cuba could live with Kennedy: "In the last analysis, I'm convinced that anyone else would be worse." Then he added, "If you see him again, tell him that I'm willing to declare Goldwater [the hard right challenger] my friend, if that will guarantee his re-election."

He asked Daniel to stay a few more days. The press in the U.S. was reporting a relatively conciliatory speech Kennedy had made the day before over Latin American policy and Cuba. But Kennedy never got to hear of Fidel's response to his overtures.

Was it a madman? A Vietnamese? A member of the Ku Klux Klan? Fidel speculated aloud to Daniel as the two absorbed the news of Kennedy's shooting. As news came through that he had been assassinated, Fidel said to the journalist, "Well, there's the end of your mission of peace." Then he asked, "Who is this Lyndon Johnson? What is his reputation?" His concern over the political leanings of the new president was understandable. The presidential elections were a year away. The presence of the arch-conservative contender Barry Goldwater meant that, as Fidel predicted, Cuba was again going to be a major issue in the campaign. Johnson was not going to be outflanked on the right. He told a meeting of the state department that "the most urgent business" was what he called communist infiltration of the Western hemisphere. Less than a month after Kennedy's shooting Johnson approved the Foreign Assistance Act. It banned foreign aid for any government which did not take "appropriate steps" to enforce the blockade on Cuba. Many further such acts were to follow down the decades.

Could there have been a rapprochement had Kennedy lived? Fidel clearly believed such a development was plausible. How long it would have lasted, however, is another matter. As Fidel indicated to Daniel, U.S. hostility to the Cuban Revolution predated the explicit turn towards the socialist camp. The island stood as a beacon of progressive national liberation.

Given a free choice, how many of Latin America's millions would have opted for U.S. tutelage rather national independence and economic development freed from the overweening power of U.S. big business? Fidel remained wedded to the vision of a free continent, unified through progress as José Martí had poetically proclaimed. Sooner or later, that was always going to be at odds with a rapacious, capitalist U.S. But a thaw in relations in 1963 and 1964 might well have provided Cuba with valuable time and given Fidel room to maneuver between the tectonic plates of the two great powers in the Cold War.

Back to hostilities!

The U.S. embargo was ratcheted up another notch at the end of 1963. Fidel responded by making a second visit to the USSR, in January 1964, during which the two countries signed a five-year trade deal. As part of the negotiations Fidel endorsed the policy of peaceful co-existence.

Soon after, the seizure by the U.S. of four Cuban fishing boats for allegedly entering U.S. waters showed that co-existence was going to be anything but peaceful. Fidel responded by cutting off the water supply to the Guantánamo base. Though the fishermen were returned (and the U.S. secured independent water supplies for its base) the incident was a portent of further crises to come.

Right: **Cartoon by Ñuez in *Granma*, January 1966**
Cuba's favorite political cartoonist satirizes proceedings at the First Tricontinental Conference.

Next page: **Cuban poster**
The text reads: "We value artistic and cultural creations according to what they contribute to mankind, according to what they contribute to the vindication of mankind, to the liberation of mankind, to the happiness of mankind … There can be no aesthetic value without human content. There can be no aesthetic value that opposes justice, that opposes the wellbeing, that opposes the happiness, of mankind."

"...valoramos las creaciones culturales y artísticas en función de lo que aporten al hombre, en función de lo que aporten a la reivindicación del hombre, a la liberación del hombre, a la felicidad del hombre..."

'...No puede haber valor estético sin contenido humano. No puede haber valor estético contra la justicia, contra el bienestar, contra la felicidad, del hombre..."

Fidel Castro

INSTITUTO VENEZOLANO CUBANO DE AMISTAD — CARACAS

We have a country in which everyone has learned to read and write, in which almost a million adults are studying, a country that is the master of its resources, the master of its lands.

Left: **National School of Soils, 1964**
Fidel talking with students at one of many technical and research institutes established in the early years of the Revolution.
Next page: **El Caldero, Pico Turquino, Sierra Maestra, 1965**
Fidel with the first doctors to graduate in the Sierra Maestra.

Transforming Cuban agriculture

October 1963 saw the enacting of the Third Agrarian Reform, which limited private land holdings to 168 acres. From that moment Fidel threw himself tirelessly into raising agricultural productivity across the island. In Paris Naty Revuelta, now science attaché to the Cuban Embassy, secured the services of first rate scientists to assist Cuba.

They included the agronomist André Voisin, whose expertise was in cattle rearing. Fidel wanted Cuba to become self-sufficient in dairy produce. That meant enormous effort in producing a breed that could withstand tropical conditions. He buried himself in the detail, not for the first time astonishing experts with his grasp of technicalities that were normally the preserve of the distinguished readership of abstruse scientific journals. His enthusiasm and confidence were total. They extended even to him trying to persuade Voisin that Cuban Camembert was, in fact, superior to the French classic!

Left: **Matanzas province, January 1965**
Fidel with a group of French agricultural specialists visiting a sugarcane field. 1965 was named the Year of Agriculture, and Fidel led efforts to find scientific and technical ways to raise efficiency and productivity.

Che's revolutionary pathway

In the big public meetings, one can observe something like the dialog of two tuning forks whose vibrations summon forth new vibrations in the other. Fidel and the mass begin to vibrate in a dialog of growing intensity which reaches its culminating point in an abrupt ending crowned by our victorious battle cry.

Those words from Che's *Man and Socialism in Cuba* convey not only the symbiosis between a great orator and the audience, but between Che and Fidel—the "brains" and the "heart" of the Revolution—themselves. As Che put it, Fidel proceeded by an "intuitive method." It was often Che who fleshed out theoretically the course of the Revolution.

Fidel's often uneasy alliance with orthodox Communism inside and outside Cuba was not just a product of his strong minded sense of independence and commitment to the revolutionary process in the Third World, whatever the diplomatic relations between the U.S. and USSR. It also reflected his rejection of stale and fatalist accounts of history and politics. He and Che believed that the Revolution could make a huge stride forward in creating a "new man," one who was motivated by moral incentives to better society rather than by the prospect of material gain.

Of course, both Fidel and Che were aware of the circumstances in which they operated, in Cuba and internationally. But their instinct was to push against the barriers of reality rather than accommodate them. Representatives of revolutionary movements, from Palestine to Vietnam, became frequent visitors to Havana. In February 1965

Che made an incendiary speech in Algiers criticizing the Soviets for failing to give adequate support to the Third World revolution. After he returned to Cuba, Che disappeared from the world stage. Speculation mounted that he had fallen from favor; in fact he had secretly flown to the former Belgian Congo where he took to the mountains to help launch a guerrilla insurrection modeled on the victorious one Fidel had led. Tragically, he found the Congolese rebels far less determined than his Cuban guerrillas. In Cuba, the ruling party changed its name to the Cuban Communist Party in October 1965. Che's name was not on the list of central committee members. To quash rumors of a split, Fidel read out a letter written by his friend on his departure for Congo six months earlier. It read:

Other nations call for my modest support. I can do what you are unable to do because of your position as the leader of Cuba. The time has come for us to part ... If my final hour finds me under other skies, my first thoughts will be of this people and especially of you ... I embrace you with all my revolutionary fervor, Che.

Not long after, Che returned to Havana, disguised as a foreign businessman. Typically, the failure of the Congo expedition had not deterred him. He was deployed to launch the "Andean project," an attempt to trigger a guerrilla struggle in Argentina, Peru, and Bolivia. He went to Bolivia, with 17 other Cuban revolutionaries, to strike a blow in the strategic center of South America—a daring revolutionary venture that was finally to cost him his life.

Next page: **Silkscreen of Fidel and Che by René Mederos**

Down with the imperialists!

While Che was operating abroad, Fidel sought to galvanize an anti-imperialist bloc by holding the First Tri-Continental Conference of Africa, Asia and Latin America in Havana in 1966. In so clearly linking the struggles in Vietnam and Africa to those in the Americas, he was directly challenging the U.S. doctrine that it could do as it pleased in its own backyard of the Western hemisphere. It also brought Fidel into conflict with those elements of the Latin American left which had forsaken revolutionary struggle in favor of a gradual, constitutionalist path.

He clashed with the leaders of the Venezuelan Communist Party, who accused him of fomenting a faction in favor of armed struggle. Fidel carried his message to millions of young radicals through the book *Revolution within the Revolution,* written by French intellectual Régis Debray after long interviews with the Cuban leader. Fidel even had Debray spirited into Bolivia to meet Che. But hopes for Bolivia becoming a second Vietnam were brutally crushed when Che—isolated and betrayed—was captured and murdered in October 1967.

Fidel was devastated by the news. According to Celia Sánchez, he took to his room and punched and kicked the walls. The U.S. and its apologists were jubilant at Che's execution. Staid leftists who preferred pontificating to action barely suppressed their satisfaction that an impatient revolutionary had fallen foul of the "objective, iron laws" of historical development. They had no inkling that in death Che was to provide inspiration for wave after wave of radical struggle the world over. But in the immediate aftermath, one consequence was to leave Fidel more dependent on Soviet backing.

Domestically, he moved to clamp down on the petty profiteering that threatened efforts to direct the economy and also provided a base for a counter-revolutionary minority to develop.

Looking back on the period decades later, Fidel and the Cuban leadership admitted that mistakes were made. While unveiling a statue of John Lennon in May 2003, Fidel described the two years in which the Beatles music was banned in Cuba as "one of the greatest cultural errors of the Revolution." Few present even recalled that the ban had been in place. Fidel, however, was not prepared to conceal the unpleasant fact.

By the end of the decade, there was no escaping the facts, however unpalatable. The gains of the Revolution were remarkable and ensured that it retained deep popular support. Across the island children went to school, where they received free meals—a feat still not achieved by many advanced capitalist nations. Medical care, which had previously been available only to the well heeled, was now of a superb standard and free to the whole population.

A population that had been split by racism and the legacy of slavery had taken huge strides towards José Martí's ideal of a true brotherhood of man. Yet, there were shortages. In the absence of material incentives, moral incentives to raise output only went so far. Moreover, Fidel was concerned at the cancer of bureaucratic inefficiency that Che had railed against in the Soviet system.

All the objective laws beloved of armchair socialists suggested that this daring experiment could not survive. But far from retreating, Fidel threw all his personal authority into fighting back against these difficulties. His method of popular, direct appeal to the Cuban people was central to the struggle to secure the economic foundation of the Revolution. And, as the Revolution reached its tenth anniversary in January 1969, Fidel had far from given up on the goal of placing Cuba at the service of global radical change.

PRIMER

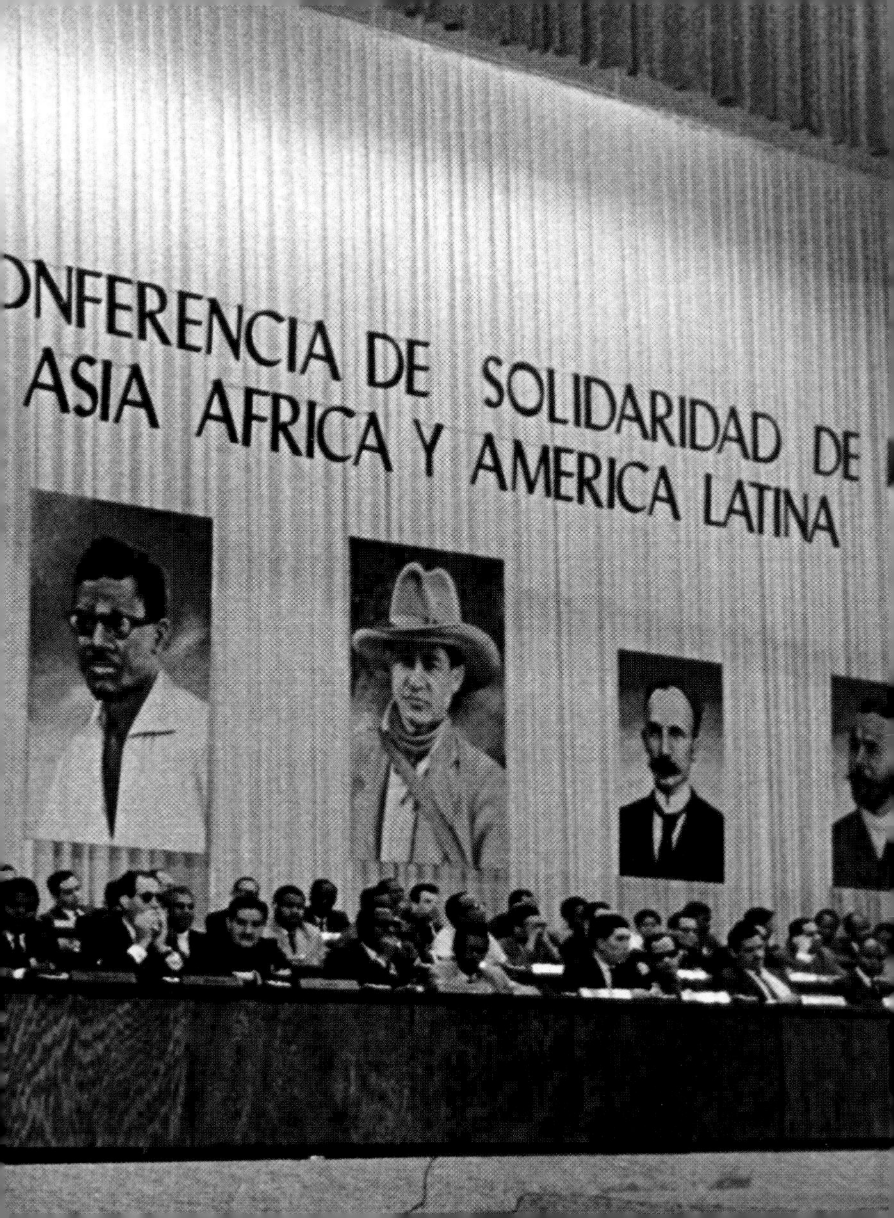
ONFERENCIA DE SOLIDARIDAD DE
ASIA AFRICA Y AMERICA LATINA

How close we could look into a bright future should two, three, or many Vietnams flourish throughout the world ... Our every action is a battle cry against imperialism, and a battle hymn for the people's unity against the great enemy of mankind: the United States of America.

Che Guevara

Previous page: **Havana, January 1966**

In the final session of the First Conference of Solidarity with the Peoples of Asia, Africa and Latin America, Fidel proclaimed 1966 the "Year of Solidarity" and made common cause with the guerrilla struggles taking place against imperialism around the world. A year later Che Guevara, already fighting in Bolivia, sent his last message to the Tricontinental organization created at the conference, in which he foresaw that the fight of the Vietnamese against the half million strong U.S. invasion force would lead to the defeat of U.S. imperialism.

Left: **Havana, June 1969**

Demonstration of solidarity with the people of Vietnam on the occasion of Tran Buu Kiem's visit to Cuba. During the visit Cuba accredited Vietnam's first ambassador to Cuba.

Sugar: the heart of the economy

Sugar was still at the center of the Cuban economy and Fidel mobilized the whole nation at the end of the decade in an effort to secure a 10 million ton harvest for the first time in Cuba's history.

He understood that something which might seem mundane in comparison with the epoch-making events of the 1960s—the amount of sugar Cuba produced—had in fact become the linchpin of his relations with the Soviet Union, the U.S. and the world as a whole.

The side-lining of Khrushchev in 1964 and his replacement by Leonid Brezhnev created new complications for Fidel. While he had never forgiven Khrushchev for timidity during the Missile Crisis and failure to openly support the nascent revolutionary movement in Latin America, Fidel nevertheless considered him a friend. He kept his own counsel over the change at the top in Moscow and held out some hope that the new leadership might be more willing to offer support to Third World revolutionaries.

Right: **Havana province, 1969**
Fidel setting an example cutting sugarcane during the attempt to reach the target of 10 million tons in the 1969–70 harvest.

chapter 6

Leading the Third World

Principled pragmatism: 1970–1991

Fidel declared 1970 the year of the 10 million tons. As a milestone in the drive to break out of economic dependency his aim was to achieve the largest sugar harvest in Cuban history. "The 10 million ton harvest represents far more than tons of sugar, far more than an economic victory," he told the *Granma* newspaper in October 1969. "It is a test, a moral duty for this country … we cannot fall a single gram short of the 10 million … Even one pound below the 10 million tons—we say this before the whole world—would be a defeat, not a victory." He saw reaching the target as akin to a military engagement, and said of troops mobilized to go to the fields:

We want the soldiers to act as though the enemy were invading our coast, as they would in the midst of war, with all the heroism, all the valor and tenacity, all the abnegation of men defending their flag.

He spurred on the population throughout the extended harvest period that lasted up to July 1970 through an endless barrage of statistics and, typically, leading by example—often working four hours a day in the enervating heat of the cane fields. But the entire drive came up against problems with ramshackle equipment, capricious weather and the burden of inherited patterns of corruption at management level and questionable commitment from large numbers of laborers. The considerable harvest of 8.5 million tons was declared by Fidel, with painful honesty, a failure. He readily took responsibility for it and set about a series of economic reforms designed to address the productivity weaknesses.

The battle of the 10 million was not lost by the people, it is us, the administrative apparatus, the leaders of the revolution who lost it. Most of the time we fell into the error of minimizing the complexity of the problems facing us.

Fidel acknowledged that it had been an illusion to believe that Cuba could become "at a stroke, a society in which everyone behaved in an ethical and moral fashion." He moved to reintroduce material incentives for work, aimed at cutting dangerous levels of absenteeism. But it soon became evident that the overwhelming focus on the sugarcane harvest had left other sectors of agriculture and industry in Cuba neglected and damaged.

One consequence of all this was that Fidel had to turn even more to the Soviet Union for economic support. In May 1972 he traveled to Moscow for the first time in eight years. Cuba was accepted as the ninth member of the Council for Mutual Economic Aid (COMECON) and was included in trading arrangements of the Soviet Union and Eastern Europe. Fidel described the agreement as giving "extraordinary concessions" to Cuba. The price of Cuban sugar sold to the socialist bloc doubled. Cuba was granted a moratorium on debt and given further loans. By the mid-1970s the global price of sugar had risen. For Cubans the decade became the "golden seventies".

Previous page: **Plaza de la Revolución, Havana, January 1, 1970**
Celebration of the eleventh anniversary of the Revolution.
Next page: **"¡Los 10 millones van!," Havana, 1970**
Volunteer cane cutters for the attempted 10 million ton harvest.

Fidel and Allende: the Chilean revolution

We have had no rest for our body, our voice, or our soul during these splendid days. We have been highly interested in extending our visit, so not a single place will complain, be displeased, or feel neglected or forgotten.

Fidel's visit to Salvador Allende's Chile on November 10, 1971 lasted into December—25 days in all. But as he traveled the length of the country—right down to Punta Arenas, the most southerly city in the world—he detected that although Allende's Popular Unity coalition formed the government, it was anything but the Chilean leader's country. Fidel was in Chile during the first serious attempt by the right to mobilize extra-parliamentary opposition to the government, which had won a slim majority the previous year.

He warned his friend Allende darkly of the dangers inherent in not proceeding apace to dismantle counter-revolutionary opposition. For Fidel, the election of a radically reforming government in Chile offered the chance for Cuba to break out of U.S. imposed isolation in the hemisphere and held out the prospect of the two countries offering a lead across the continent. "The stars of Cuba and Chile shall go forward to illuminate the path of Latin American revolution," he told the Moncada anniversary rally in 1971.

Allende had come to power in Chile not through guerrilla struggle, but through a European-style parliamentary election. He had made radical socialist reforms, including nationalizing the big mining companies.

Above: **Valparaíso, Chile, November 1971**

Chilean president Salvador Allende (holding hat), Fidel, Luis Corvalán and Carlos Altamirano.

Allende's fears that his friend might go over the top in his rhetoric in front of large left wing crowds proved groundless. Fidel, in fact, preached moderation to the extreme left and called for an alliance behind Allende alongside followers of liberation Catholicism and progressive elements of the middle class.

When asked about the apparent differences between the Cuban and Chilean roads to socialism, he said:

Not only did we find no contradiction, we will always look with satisfaction on every new variation that may appear. And let every variation in the world make its appearance!
If all roads lead to Rome, we can only wish for thousands of roads to revolutionary Rome!

Left: **Lota coal mine, Chile, November 24, 1971**
Fidel speaking with coal miners.

Travels through Chile

Fidel visited scores of factories, farms, and most of Chile's major cities. He laid wreaths at memorials to Chilean independence leader Bernardo O'Higgins, to José Martí and, poignantly, to Che—the latter erected in a shanty-town. Diplomatic niceties meant that, as prime minister rather than head of state, Fidel was not meant to make impromptu speeches but to stick to an agreed schedule. Protocol broke down almost instantly.

He gave countless speeches, often to students and young people. He was up early and often still meeting ordinary Chileans late into the night. He explained to students the philosophy behind the educational revolution that was unfolding in Cuba.

To educate is to prepare man from the time he begins to reason, so he can live up to his obligations to society—to produce the material and spiritual goods that society needs and to produce them equally, everyone with the same obligation.

And, as usual, he astonished audiences with his grasp of detail about Chile and its economy. His abiding concern was to explain the process that was underway in Cuba and to strengthen support for the Popular Unity government in Chile. So, while he held firm to the path that had brought the Cuban revolution to power, he acknowledged that Allende's electoral struggle had also borne fruit. Nevertheless, both faced the antagonism of the U.S. and the machinations of domestic counter-revolutionary forces. He urged the most radical elements of the left not to break unity with Allende.

Equally, he appealed to the more moderate democratic elements, which were similar to those liberal figures who had supported the Cuban revolution in its early stages.

Fidel held out the prospect of an alliance between the peoples of Latin America. "We try to share our music, our literature, our traditions, our knowledge," he said of Cuba's role. Allende, in return, said, "If he is here with us, it is because he is aware that we are also undertaking a revolution, and that each nation confronts such a challenge in accordance with its own reality." The realities were not so dissimilar. The Chilean government, despite its constitutional validity, was beset by counter-revolutionary opposition just as Cuba's had been. Fidel's presence highlighted the coming struggle.

On December 1 a few thousand upper class women and their maids took to the streets of Santiago banging empty pots in an orchestrated protest against shortages, which were the product of the U.S. frustrating imports into Chile. Fidel's visit was a major focus of their chants. The protest was small, but so too, by Cuban standards, was the turnout by Popular Unity supporters for set-piece rallies. The right wing agitation triggered significant violence in the capital—a sign of much worse in the two years to come.

Allende felt confident even so, saying at a farewell rally for Fidel that "only by riddling my body with bullets" could his opponents undermine the program he had been elected on. In any case, the security of the capital was in safe hands—he had given the job to the commander of the city's garrison, Augusto Pinochet. Fidel confided in Cuban officials that he was staggered at the illusions of the Popular Unity leadership in the supposed neutrality of the army. His fears were tragically justified when none other than Pinochet led the U.S. sponsored coup two years later which claimed the lives of Allende and over 5,000 Chilean leftists, workers and students.

Allende made a reciprocal visit to Havana in December 1972. It was his last. On 11 September 1973 he was overthrown in a CIA-supported coup. What the U.S. and the Chilean upper classes had found intolerable was not only Allende's domestic reforms, but also his alliance with Fidel and the possibility of the two forming the corner stones of an independent, progressive bloc of Latin American nations. "The problem in Chile was not Allende," said CIA Director Colby, "It was Fidel Castro."

This first 9/11—the coup of September 11, 1973—was a terrible blow for the international left and prompted much soul-searching. In many circles the conclusion drawn was that Allende had gone too far, too quickly. For Fidel, it was the opposite. The government had not pressed its early advantage and moved to disorganize the forces ranged against it. And it had not sought to arm the people against the threat of a coup.

Cuba became the sanctuary for large numbers of Chilean exiles. Fidel followed events in Chile after the coup closely and warned that unless there was mighty resistance to it, the Popular Unity coalition would be no more and the left would be marginalized for a generation. It took more than a generation for the left to return to center stage in Latin America.

Right: **Cuban poster with faces of President Salvador Allende and Fidel**
"Chile and Cuba—We will overcome."
Next page: **Havana, June 1973**
Fidel with delegates to the X International Festival of Students and Youth.

CHILE Y CUBA

VENCEREMOS

The Non-Aligned Movement

In May 1972, Fidel set out on a two-month international tour that showed how he was prioritizing building international alliances. He traveled to Algeria, where he walked to the Palace of the People down the broad Che Guevara Avenue. In Eastern Europe and the Soviet Union Fidel was the perfect guest, but in private he urged the leaders to do more to help the Vietnamese struggle. If Cuba, a small nation under blockade, could play its part in international solidarity, then why not the more developed states of Eastern Europe?

While a close ally of the Soviet Union, Fidel was also part of the Non-Aligned Movement. The ire that aroused among some of the movement's other members came to a head at its fourth summit in September 1973, for which Fidel again traveled to Algiers. In opposition to those who spoke of "Soviet imperialism," he said imperialist aggression came not from the East but the West.

Libya's Colonel Qaddafi responded, "There is no difference between Cuba and an Eastern European country, just as there is no difference between the Soviet Union and Uzbekistan. The difference between me and Castro is that he is a communist, and I am a socialist; he is aligned, and I am not."

What followed showed not only Fidel's preparedness to act against the wishes of the Soviet leadership, but also his capacity to change his mind over major issues. The struggle of the Palestinians had encouraged him towards a more and more critical attitude to Israel. He announced to the conference that he was breaking off diplomatic relations with the Zionist state, something no member of the Soviet bloc had done. His argument was a model of clarity in distinguishing between the Jewish people and the Israeli state:

"We repudiate with all our strength the ruthless persecution and genocide that Nazism unleashed in its time against the Jewish people. But there is nothing more similar in contemporary history than the eviction, persecution and genocide being carried out by imperialism and Zionism against the Palestinian people. Piece by piece the Palestinian lands, and territories belonging to neighboring Arab countries, have been seized by the aggressors, who are armed to the teeth with the most sophisticated weapons of the United States arsenal. United Nations resolutions have been contemptuously ignored or rejected by the aggressors and their imperialist allies. Can anyone doubt that the United States plays a fundamental role in preventing a just settlement in the region, by aligning itself with Israel, by supporting it, by working towards partial solutions that favor Zionist objectives, and by safeguarding the fruits of Israeli aggression at the expense of the Palestinian people?"

Fidel's move had a considerable impact in making Cuba a point of reference for the anti-imperialist movement in the Arab and Muslim worlds. Similarly, his unflinching support for the liberation movement in Angola won plaudits even from anti-communist African leaders. But the overthrow of Allende underscored the resourcefulness of the old order.

He told the East German leader Eric Honecker five months after the coup, "Since my visit to Chile, I had seen the strength of reaction, the fascism, the government's weaknesses and its powerlessness. I had the impression that the government's only chance of saving itself was to go on the offensive, a mass popular offensive … I think that in that situation the only option was to try to arm the popular forces. Naturally it would have been dangerous, but it was more dangerous to do nothing."

Yasser Arafat is a man we deeply love and admire and to whom we have always shown our solidarity.

Fidel Castro, 1975

The people of Cuba ... have made us feel that we form part of one long worldwide struggle

Yasser Arafat, 1974

Right: **Havana, September 1974**
Cuban president Osvaldo Dorticós decorating Palestinian Liberation Organization president Yasser Arafat with the Order of the Bay of Pigs.

The colonialists had thought that Algerian petroleum would not flow without them, but now production has increased, new gas pipelines are being constructed ...

Left: **Algiers, Algeria, September 1973**
With Algerian president Houari Boumédienne (left) at the IV Summit of the Non-Aligned Movement. Fidel went on to visit Iraq, India and Vietnam.

We went swimming in the rivers, running through the woods ... We lived in direct contact with nature and were quite free during these times. That's what my childhood was like.

Right: **Sofia, Bulgaria, May 1972**

Fidel enjoying a swim—one of his favorite relaxations. This reminds me of the time when I accompanied him on a midnight swim during one of our late-night conversations. He likes to meet people at night and talk into the early hours. Once I met him at 1 A.M. and we talked until dawn.

Soviet influence grows

A period of détente between the two superpowers meant that the U.S. by the middle of the decade showed a marked reluctance to enforce the economic blockade of Cuba in its entirety. There was a spirit of optimism in Havana when Leonid Brezhnev paid a week-long visit in January 1974. Fidel had feared that détente would leave the U.S. emboldened to strike against Cuba, but the Americans were catastrophically bogged down in Vietnam.

Within Cuba, the early 1970s were marked by a turn toward Soviet cultural and social policy. Looking back later, Fidel and other leaders criticized the excesses of the period. In particular, there were clashes with some of the intellectuals who had given support for the Revolution, but who were being lauded abroad as a possible organizing focus against the government, especially as it leant heavily on the Soviet model. The arrest of the poet Heberto Padilla in 1971 brought condemnation from an array of left wing European and Latin American writers.

Fidel met Padilla privately and persuaded him to recant. The whole affair meant some of the intellectual fellow travelers of the Revolution departed for good. But many, including Gabriel García Márquez, maintained a fundamental commitment to Cuba and to Fidel, recognizing that reality is much more complex than the imaginary, and that the latitude the Revolution could display within Cuba always depended on the strength of the pressures it faced from outside.

Right: **Havana International Airport, January 28, 1974**
Soviet president Leonid Brezhnev arriving for a week's visit.

We want to improve relations ... (But) we could resist the blockade for another 15 years.

Left: **Havana, April 1975**
U.S. Senator George
McGovern with Fidel,
answering questions from
foreign press. McGovern had
run unsuccessfully for the U.S.
presidency as the Democratic
Party candidate in 1972.

317

Angola: slaves return as liberators

Angola won its independence as a result of a revolution in Portugal, its colonial overlord, in 1974. An accord between three rival Angolan forces in January 1975 was supposed to lead to free elections by November of that year. "One might have expected the U.S. to back [the accord] to the full," wrote former State Department official Wayne Smith. "Instead, incredibly, the Ford administration moved to do the exact opposite."

The Marxist MPLA movement, led by Agostinho Neto, was a shoo-in for the planned elections. The U.S., smarting from defeat in Vietnam, thought it could draw a new line in Angola. It threw its support behind the MPLA's rivals, and in particular UNITA, plunging Angola into two decades of carnage that would shock the world, before being written off as some "tribal conflict" unrelated to the actions of the world's imperialist powers.

For Fidel, support for the MPLA and the struggle of the Angolan people was not only a political question, but a moral imperative. "We are a Latin-African nation; African blood flows through our veins," he said, referring to the peopling of the island through the slave trade three centuries before. He gave the Angolan operation the code name Carlota after the famous female leader of a slave uprising in Cuba in the nineteenth century. U.S. allies in the invasion of Angola included the murderous regime in Zaire and apartheid South Africa. "The Angolans asked us for help," said Fidel, "Angola was invaded by South Africa. Therefore we could never have done anything more than just to help Angola against an external invasion."

By October 1975 there were 1,500 Cuban troops in Angola. Fidel deployed them despite the confrontation it would mean with the U.S. and the consequent diplomatic difficulties it might create with the Soviet Union. The left wing Jamaican prime minister, Michael Manley, wrote:

"Fidel told me privately that he judged the Russians couldn't do anything after he moved into Angola … When the Cuban soldiers were set to fly across the Atlantic, Raúl was on a plane to Moscow. He found the Soviets so infuriated at what he had done that it took two days to calm them down."

By February 1976 there were 15,000 Cubans serving in Angola. In the years that followed there were as many as 40,000 at a time. Over 200,000 Cuban soldiers fought there over a period of 16 years, ending in 1991. Fidel himself oversaw operations from a command post in Havana and mastered the most obscure facts about the country's terrain.

The Cuban presence brought swift victories to the MPLA forces. The significance of the combined forces of Cuba, three-quarters of whose troops were black, and the MPLA routing the shock troops of apartheid was not lost even on those African leaders who were bitterly critical of Fidel.

The campaign ranks as one of the finest acts of internationalism in history. But it dragged on and the Angolan leadership proved less scrupulous and dedicated than the Cubans. The costs in human and economic terms to Cuba were great—Fidel gave both troops and doctors for very little in return for their sacrifices.

The turning point came in 1988 at Cuito Cuanavale. Fidel by then was spending, by his own account, 80 percent of his time on Angola. He took an interest in the smallest details of the defense of Cuito Cuanavale, right down to the soldiers' rations. In February 1988, 35,000 UNITA and 9,000 South African troops attacked, supported by tanks and aircraft. The Cuban-Angolan front lines were breached.

The defense held, however, and the pro-imperialist forces were hurled back. Cuito Cuanavale went down in history as the engagement that marked the beginning of the end of the Angolan war, and of the apartheid regime. It left Fidel deeply angered at the timidity of the then Soviet leader Mikhail Gorbachev, who refused to support the Cubans going on the offensive after the battle and instead orchestrated talks leading to the removal of all "foreign armies." It was the kind of caution from Moscow that had worried Fidel over the decades—though, perhaps this time, there was even more of it. "We are left with the honor of being one of the few adversaries of the United States," he told U.S. reporter Maria Shriver, a relative of John F Kennedy. It hadn't seemed so lonely when Fidel first ordered troops to Angola.

Cuba did pay a price for that decision in 1975. The U.S. position hardened as Fidel frustrated its plans in Angola. On 6 October 1976 a Cuban airliner was blown up just after taking off from Barbados. The attack by ultra-right Cubans, evidently with CIA support, claimed the lives of 73 people. Even so, in September 1977 limited diplomatic relations were restored for the first time in 16 years with "representation of interests" bureaux set up in Havana and Washington, D.C. Then, suddenly, President Carter announced that talks would be broken off unless Cuba disengaged from Angola. Fidel did not hesitate to reject the demand out of hand.

Left: **Angola, 1976**
Cuban and Angolan troops during a visit by the Cuban High Command.
Next page: **Street murals, Angola**
Portuguese text (left): "Whatever it costs, the people's revolution will triumph." Spanish text (right): "Socialism is the highest form of justice."

¡EL SOCIALISMO ES LA FORMA SUPERIOR DE JUSTICIA...!

Fidel's words to the world

Fidel's internationalism was expressed not primarily through military alliances, but through medical, educational, and other civilian support for some of the poorest or least developed countries in the world. By 1979 an astonishing 35 countries were receiving such support from Cuba, itself an embattled and poor nation. Cuban doctors and teachers were at work on every continent. At home they provided a quality of education and health care that was the envy of not just the Third World, but of many in the advanced capitalist countries where such services were priced out of reach of the poor.

Fidel always saw the moral dimension of politics. His most memorable speeches draw not on the lexicon of international affairs, but on the basic moral oppositions that more deeply shape the world. So, speaking at the UN General Assembly in October 1979, he identified the brute statistics of what would become known as the debt trap, through which the blood of millions in the Third World was drained into Western banks. His harshest rhetoric was reserved for the grotesque immorality behind the balance sheets.

Fidel addressed the General Assembly in the name of the Non-Aligned Movement. The month before he had hosted the movement's sixth summit, at which 94 states and liberation movements had participated. Fidel, now aged 53, had placed Cuba at the forefront of world affairs.

Left: **United Nations General Assembly, New York, October 12, 1979**
Fidel speaking as president of the Movement of Non-Aligned Countries.

There is often talk of human rights, but it is also necessary to talk of the rights of humanity. Why should some people walk barefoot so that others can travel in luxurious cars? Why should some live for 35 years, so that others can live for 70 years? Why should some be miserably poor, so that others can be hugely rich?

I speak on behalf of the children of the world who do not have even a piece of bread. I speak on behalf of the sick who have no medicine, of those whose rights to life and human dignity have been denied...What is the destiny of the latter? To starve to death? To be eternally poor? What use than is civilization? What's the use of man's conscience? What's the use of the United Nations? What's the use of the world? We can't speak of peace when tens of millions of human beings die every year of hunger, or of curable diseases. Enough of words and abstractions.

Actions are needed. I ask the rich countries to contribute. I ask the poor countries to distribute what they have. I have not come as a prophet of revolution. I don't want violent upheaval. I am here to ask for peace and co-operation among nations. I am here to warn that either injustice and inequalities are resolved peacefully and wisely, or the future will be apocalyptic. The sound of weapons, and of threatening words, must cease.

The world's problems cannot be solved with nuclear weapons. Bombs can kill the hungry, the sick and the ignorant, but they cannot kill hunger, disease, ignorance or the people's just rebellion. In a holocaust, the rich will also die. They have most to lose. Let us try to solve the world's problems in a civilized way. That is our responsibility, and the indispensable requirement for mankind's survival.

Globalizing the revolution

In 1977 Fidel sent troops to support Ethiopia in its border dispute with Somalia, where President Mohammed Siad Barre had switched to the pro-U.S. camp in order to secure backing for his invasion of the Ogaden province. The luster was coming off many of the states which, in words at any rate, had seemed committed to a progressive, anti-imperialist order.

At the same time, Fidel persuaded three opposition groups in Nicaragua to come together under the banner of the Sandinista Liberation Front to fight the dictator Anastasio Somoza. Upon his fall in July 1979, Fidel sent hundreds of teachers and doctors to assist the revolutionary reconstruction. Military and security advisors helped the new government secure power. When Fidel visited Nicaragua he reminded his audience that the country was the departure point for the Bay of Pigs invasion two decades before.

Luis Somoza, Anastasio's father and the then dictator, had told the CIA's Brigade 2506 to bring back a hair from Fidel's beard. Not only was the beard still intact, said Fidel, it was now in Nicaragua—with the Somoza dictatorship in exile.

Right: **Nicaragua, January 10, 1985**
While visiting Nicaragua for the investiture of Daniel Ortega (right) as president, Fidel received the order of Augusto Cesar Sandino.

The most honest, courageous politician I have ever met.

Jesse Jackson on Fidel, 1984

Left: **Havana, June 26, 1984**
Rev. Jesse Jackson visited Cuba for three days during the year that he stood for the Democratic party nomination for U.S. president.

For Castro, freedom
begins with education.

Barbara Walters, NBC presenter

Right: **Havana, 1988**
The U.S. television presenter Barbara Walters visited Cuba to interview
Fidel for transmission by the NBC network.
Following page: **Havana, 1980**
Fidel speaking in celebration of the USSR-Cuba Cosmos space flight in
which Yuri Romanenko of the Soviet Union and Arnaldo Tamayo Méndez
of Cuba participated. "Eternal Friendship" was to last another eleven years.

The demise of the Soviet Union

The leviathan of neo-liberalism was stalking the globe at the dawn of the 1980s. By the middle of the decade Mikhail Gorbachev had introduced into the Soviet Union the market mechanisms that would tear the state apart. In the new climate, attempts by the Sandinistas in Nicaragua to accommodate the bloodstained forces of the right led to the fall of their government at the end of the decade.

Fidel told his friend Gabriel García Márquez that the course followed by Gorbachev would lead to disaster years before the collapse came. When the Soviet leader visited Havana in April 1989, he was confronted by a gigantic banner reading, "Long live Marxism-Leninism!" It was a defiant act and also a call for Gorbachev to acknowledge that Cuba was taking a different path. Within two years the Warsaw pact and the Soviet Union itself were no more. It was a massive blow to Cuba, which was already beset by economic travails. The prospect of finding allies in Latin America seemed as remote as ever. Trading arrangements with the Soviet Union had already deteriorated severely under Gorbachev, now they were barely extant. In 1992 a *Miami Herald* journalist published a best-selling book called *Castro's Final Hour.* Surely it was only a matter of months, a few years at most?

Right: **Moscow, November 1987**
During a visit to Moscow for the 70th anniversary celebrations of the Russian Revolution Fidel met Soviet president Mikhail Gorbachev for the first time.

Sanctuary for Chernobyl's victims

Cuba was one of the first to extend a helping hand with health care for the children.

Ukrainian health minister, 2005

Cuba became a haven for thousands of children who were victims of the Chernobyl nuclear disaster in 1986. As the USSR began to fall apart, Cuba stepped in to provide free health care for fallout victims from 1990 onwards. In the following 15 years, over 18,000 Ukrainian children were treated in Cuba at the beach resort of Tarará.

In 2005 Ukrainian health minister Nykola Polischuk led a delegation to Havana to thank Fidel and the Cuban government for the program. Ukrainian children danced on stage and recited poems by José Martí.

Left: **Havana, July 2, 1990**
Fidel receiving Ukrainian children suffering the effects of radiation from the Chernobyl nuclear reactor disaster. The children came to Cuba for treatment at the Tarará Paediatric Hospital at East Havana beach. In the following years some 22,000 Chernobyl children and adults were to come to Cuba for treatment.

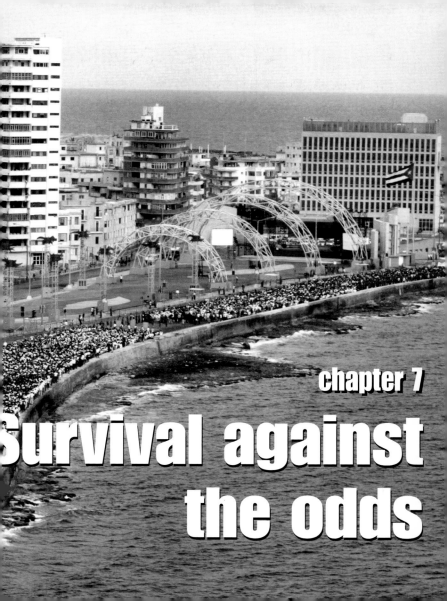

chapter 7

Survival against the odds

Cuba prevails! 1991–the present

We warn imperialism that it shouldn't have so many illusions about our Revolution, thinking that our revolution won't be able to stand firm if there's a catastrophe in the socialist community. If, tomorrow or another day, we should wake up to the news that a huge civil war has broken out in the Soviet Union or even that the Soviet Union has disintegrated, Cuba and the Cuban Revolution would keep on struggling and keep on standing firm.

Prophetic defiance was Fidel's message on July 26, 1989. Two years later, the Soviet Union was indeed no more and Cuba would be plunged into the most arduous period since the Revolution. The increasingly powerful ultra-right Cuban businessmen in Miami were salivating, as were all those who had never forgiven Fidel for keeping Cuba outside the clutches of imperialist domination.

They believed they were finally to see the back of the leader Richard Nixon had dubbed the "bastard" of the Caribbean. Such were the expectations when Havana hosted the Pan-American Games in August 1991. A record 1,300 foreign journalists attended. Some were sports correspondents; many were sent by foreign desks, hoping to witness a "Ceausescu moment", in which the Cuban people would use the opportunity of the games to turn violently against Fidel, just as the Romanians had transformed a staged rally into a movement to topple their ruler two years previously. They expected to find half-built stadiums and amateurish organization of the games, and they were certain that the Cuban crowds would use the presence of the foreign press to make their true feelings about Fidel known. Despite the mounting economic maelstrom engulfing Cuba as it struggled to make good the hole left by the canceled Soviet trade agreements, the facilities were completed to international standards and the games ran smoothly. There were no anti-Fidel demonstrations. Even the most jaundiced journalists had to file reports admitting that the Maximum Leader's appearances were greeted with uncoerced chants of "Fidel!"

As if to puncture further the arrogance in Washington, basking in vainglory after the war earlier that year against Iraq, Cuba's athletes turned in a brilliant performance. Cuba came top of the gold medal table, the first time a Latin American country had beaten the U.S. in an athletics competition. The Cubans were magnanimous in victory.

There were other boosts to morale, sorely needed in the embattled nation. In July 1991 Nelson Mandela spoke at the Moncada anniversary rally in Havana. It was the first foreign capital he visited as President of South Africa. Standing next to Fidel, he told the giant crowd: "See how far we slaves have come!" It was a reminder of the crucial blow Cuba had struck against apartheid at the battle of Cuito Cuanavale in Angola.

Previous page: **Havana malecón, 2006**
March in protest at the U.S. Cuban Adjustment Law, which grants residency and, within one year, citizenship to any Cuban arriving within U.S. territory and thus encourages perilous emigration.
Next page: **Havana, July 1991**
Fidel with South African president Nelson Mandela.

The coup against Gorbachev

At a diplomatic function after the Pan-American Games, Fidel heard that a group of hardliners in Moscow had executed a coup against Mikhail Gorbachev. There was tremendous excitement in Havana. Many Cuban communists believed the tide was about to turn: no more chaotic introduction of the market in the Soviet Union and instead of Gorbachev's lurch to the West, renewed support for allies such as Cuba. Iraq and Libya moved swiftly to recognize the new government; Fidel refused to leap to conclusions. He issued a statement designed to give no hostages to fortune, no matter who emerged victorious from the power struggle in Moscow.

In fact, the coup collapsed; Gorbachev returned to office, but the power behind the throne was Boris Yeltsin. That was very bad news for Cuba. Yeltsin was committed to handing Russia over to what would become the corrupt oligarchs. Worse, two years earlier he had already established friendly relations with the fanatically anti-Fidel Cuban American National Foundation (CANF). He had established an unwritten agreement with the CANF—they would lobby on his behalf in the U.S., he would end all assistance to Cuba should he come to power in Moscow. The effective leader of what had been Fidel's strongest ally was now in alliance with an organization that had orchestrated terror attacks on Cuba and its interests, and which had been incubated in the nest of the Latin American death squads and their U.S. sponsors.

It was at least as bad as Fidel had feared when, in January 1989, he had a conversation with his old friend Gabriel García Márquez about Gorbachev's doctrine of economic restructuring—Perestroika. "Don't get me wrong, I'm not against the principles of Perestroika," said Fidel. "But it's an extremely risky policy. It's leading the socialist world back to capitalism." García Márquez thought the reforms would simply soften Soviet bureaucracy. Fidel replied, "No. Believe me, Gabo, it's going to be a disaster."

Cuba had increased its trade with the Soviet Union and Eastern Europe during the 1980s to the point where the socialist bloc accounted for over 80 percent of the island's exports. This was in response to the ferocious economic circumstances of the 1980s, a vice-like squeeze of high international interest rates and low prices for commodities, including sugar—a combination that had driven many Third World countries to ruin.

Gorbachev's internal reforms impacted on Cuba. Five-year trade deals were renegotiated to last just one year, undermining attempts to plan the island's economy for the medium term. They were signed not with the Soviet state, but with individual enterprises, which were embracing market pricing and competition. What were already often long-delayed deliveries from the Soviets now became sporadic. In the year of the Soviet Union's demise, Cuba was lucky to receive 40 percent of the goods it had been promised and had paid for through exports of sugar and nickel ore.

Fidel had long ago drawn up plans to deal with a total air and sea blockade and the dislocation that would follow a direct U.S. military attack on Cuba. It would be a "Special Period in Time of War." The sudden deterioration of international conditions now meant that Cuba faced a "Special Period in Time of Peace." It was the most testing time the Cuban people could expect short of outright war.

The Ochoa drug trafficking scandal

In 1989 Fidel faced one of the gravest and most bitter crises of the Revolution. For both him and the Cuban public it was all the more shocking and heartrending because this time the threat came from within, not from without. And it came at a time when the Soviet Union was already cutting its support for the island and the U.S. was starting to adopt a new hyper-aggressive posture.

In June of that year four senior figures were arrested on charges of corruption and drug smuggling. The number charged and brought before a tribunal eventually reached 14. Among them was General Ochoa, one of the most celebrated Cuban military leaders and the commander of the country's forces at the victory of Cuito Cuanavale in Angola. The accused also included the twin brothers Tony and Patricio de la Guardia. The flamboyant Tony de la Guardia was the head of the MC Department of the Cuban Interior Ministry. Its role was to find ways around the blockade and establish routes whereby Cuba could earn foreign currency. He had also played a pivotal role in Cuba's clandestine support for numerous guerrilla groups. Patricio had been head of special forces in Angola.

Months earlier Fidel had ordered an investigation into the group after receiving a string of complaints about their high-living and reports of Ochoa's increasingly bitter estrangement from the Cuban leadership. Raúl received a report that Ochoa had a secret bank account in Panama where he had deposited $200,000 which had been earmarked for buying equipment for the Sandinistas.

On 29 May Raúl confronted Ochoa, accusing him of unauthorized commercial deals, corruption and abuse of office. Ochoa responded that, like any good general, he had merely improvised deals to pay for extra supplies for his men. He denied he had personally enriched himself. But the investigation rapidly turned up further, more damning evidence. It centered on the involvement of the Ochoa group in drug trafficking.

The shipment of cocaine from South America to the U.S. was the great boom industry of the region in the 1980s. It was also one of the means through which death squads such as the Contras in Nicaragua obtained their funding, with the complicity of the CIA. At the apex of the drug gangs stood Pablo Escobar's Medellín cartel in Colombia. Cuba, in the middle of the Caribbean, had been strategically placed for centuries as a haven for smuggling and piracy. But Fidel had categorically refused to allow the country to be part of the drugs trade, despite the enormous financial rewards that would have brought. He explained to the *Washington Post* in 1985: "Of all the Caribbean countries, Cuba is the one that has the largest number of drug traffickers in jail. We've really become the police of the Caribbean and we often wonder why, since the U.S. doesn't pay us for this service … I assure you that we've had plenty of offers … We would practically have solved our foreign exchange problems, but we're not interested in that kind of money … I don't know whether it has to do with morals or the fact that I studied the catechism or studied all about Christian morality in Christian schools, but to me it is a question of Christian morality and Marxist-Leninist morality, and that's what we go by."

But smuggling computer and medical equipment into Cuba in defiance of the U.S. blockade did mean that Cuban agencies had to deal with the *lancheros*, the men who had the fast motor launches capable of getting round U.S. Customs. They were often also involved in the drugs trade. So the Cuban secret services were placed in a very delicate position, one which demanded the strictest standards of accountability.

Leycester Coltman, who served as British ambassador to Cuba between 1991 and 1994, wrote: "Castro suspected … that the Americans had penetrated the drugs cartels and would exploit any evidence of Cuban involvement in drug trafficking. He had given instructions that no deal should be done that involved bringing drugs onto Cuban soil or into Cuban territorial waters. When drugs arrived in Cuba by accident, there was a problem. On one occasion a boat carrying Colombian drugs to Florida strayed into Cuban waters and was arrested. The Colombians offered $1 million if it could be quietly released. Cuban officials accepted the offer but then, on Castro's orders, cancelled their acceptance. He suspected an American trap."

The U.S. Right was desperate to try to implicate Fidel and Cuba in the drugs trade. So evidence that Tony de la Guardia and Ochoa, through his *aide-de-camp,* had been involved in the trade or, at the very least, had unauthorized contact with the Medellín cartel was all the more damaging. The damage within Cuban public opinion was even greater than to the prestige of Cuba abroad. Subsequent arrests included the Interior Minister, General Abrantes, a longstanding aide to Fidel.

After a two-week trial Tony de la Guardia, Ochoa and two others were sentenced to death. Patricio de la Guardia and five others were given prison sentences of 30 years; six others got shorter terms. On July 9, 29 members of the Council of State met to ratify the verdict, then each stood up to ratify it again on television. Even hostile observers admitted that both Fidel and Raúl were deeply emotional, almost torn apart as they spoke.

Appeals for clemency flooded Fidel's office. The papal Nuncio spent two hours conveying the Pope's request for the death sentences to be commuted. Fidel's great friend Gabriel García

Márquez issued the same plea. Fidel explained that although he had considerable moral authority in Cuba the decision was not his to reverse, but had been arrived at through the due processes of the state—and, in any case, he thought the sentences just. The executions took place on July 13.

There was a predictable response from Cuba's enemies. But there was also polarization and consternation among Cuba's friends abroad and within the country itself. Many Cubans who were committed to the revolution were nevertheless stunned at the trial and executions. They saw it as an awful disfigurement of a revolution which had been in power for 30 years and of which they felt proud.

Fidel had painstakingly built up Cuba's reputation over the decades. Why should he now risk that? At the time and in interviews afterward he explained his and the Cuban leadership's actions. The Ochoa case was beyond petty corruption. In threatening to drag Cuba into the most noxious cesspits of drug trafficking, it was a treason to the revolution. What standing and future could Cuba have if, unbeknownst to the country's leaders, the country was playing host to a vile trade.

It was not just that the U.S. would have the perfect excuse for overt action against the country—the excuse it used to invade Panama later that year. It was also the irreparable damage that would be done to Cuba's role as a principled leader of the Third World. And what would happen to its capacity to appeal to the impoverished inside the U.S. itself, living in ghettos that paid the price for the drugs trade? Thus the agonizing decision. And thus a shake-up of the Interior Ministry to ensure that such a decision would not have to be made again.

Cuba's greatest test: the Special Period

The early 1990s was the period in which Fidel and Cuba arguably faced the greatest test of all. When asked about Fidel's centrality to the Cuban Revolution, many leading Cubans today will rank his role in the country's survival at that point above even the overthrow of Batista, or the defeat of the Bay of Pigs invasion.

In a speech to the Cuban people in which he candidly outlined the difficult times ahead, he deployed one of the most powerful weapons a people under siege possesses—humor. He wondered out loud what would Cuba do without those next-to-useless Bulgarian forklifts, or the Hungarian buses that seemed to consume their own weight in fuel on just a short journey? How might it survive without the delivery of snow-plows from the Soviet Union (which had actually been sent one year by mistake)? There was a palpable sense of relief from the crowd.

The Cuban leader captured their feelings and felt their concerns—like Che's tuning fork vibrating in resonance with them. But some things were unforgivable, said Fidel: what had Cuban children done to deserve the East Germans reneging on their promised delivery of powdered milk, on which the much prized delivery of free nutrition for all school students depended?

Fidel now spoke in public and toured the country more extensively than he had ever done—even in the years immediately after the revolution. He urged, he intervened, he set an example and he planned for how Cuba could survive. Hostile foreign observers were perplexed. The crescendo from Washington—under Bush the First, but continued under his successor, Bill Clinton—was barely muted in calling for the "popular" overthrow of Fidel, yet he retained a popularity that no U.S. leader could match at home. How?

First, there was the reality of what the revolution had brought to Cuba. There were shortages, but there were also welfare provision, free education, and health care. Above all, there was pride in the genuine independence Cuba had enjoyed for 40 years and for the first time in its history. What would the end of the Cuban system mean? The return of grasping millionaires from Miami, with tattered property deeds in their back pockets to enforce the eviction of countless residents in Havana as it fell back to its status as the U.S.'s Caribbean bordello. The U.S. establishment could not appeal to Cuban pride to rise up against an over-mighty superpower, for it was the U.S. itself that had played that role against the Cuban people, for a whole century.

In April 1991 Fidel appealed to the heritage of the long struggle for Cuban independence: "We will tell the imperialists, no, you can't do what you want with us! And if we have to put up with material deprivation, we will put up with it, because we can never forget that those who began our independence struggle spent ten years in the woods and when some of them got tired and thought that it was impossible to fight under such difficult conditions and wanted peace without independence, Maceo said, "No!" And, along with Maceo, the best representatives of that heroic people said, "No!" That is who we are: the heirs of Maceo, the heirs of Martí."

Secondly, there was the personality and prestige of Fidel. Whatever disappointments Cubans felt, they knew he was a million miles from the monstrous image they were bombarded with in U.S.-based radio and television broadcasts. Far from subordinating Cuba to foreign interests, he was the first leader in its history to plow an independent furrow; and in the battle to produce, he literally *did* plow. He was not remote from the people, but moved among them, and worked alongside them.

Inspiring the Cuban people

The Cuban people needed moral support, and they got it. Instead of giving tame press briefings, Fidel spoke directly to them in public— at length, and addressing the most detailed of problems. He sought to find a silver lining in every dark cloud that shrouded the island. Cuba would have to survive on half the amount of oil it was used to. So, it would import Chinese bicycles—a healthier mode of transport in any case. "In a sense this too is a revolution," said Fidel, "I have no doubt that in the summer we'll see whole clouds of cyclists heading for the beaches of our capital." Times were hard and would become harder, but they would be disastrous if the Cuban people did not, as Fidel constantly urged:

Resist! Resist! Resist!

Left: **Havana, April 4, 1992**
IV Congress of the Young Communists, held in the Conference Center. Images of Che Guevara, Antonio Mella—a founder of the Cuban Communist party—and Camilo Cienfuegos dominate the proceedings.

Fidel saw that in the medium term the way out of the economic impasse would come through two channels—high value exports of biotechnology products, which Cuba had begun to excel in during the 1980s, and tourism.

Mass tourism had negative associations for Fidel and many Cubans. In the 1940s and 1950s it had symbolized dependency and exploitation. Fidel wanted this tourism to be of a new type. But, however it was organized, it was simply an economic necessity. All this, however, was some way off.

In 1991, the question for an island used to hurricanes was how to batten down in the storm of historical events. The fourth congress of the Cuban Communist Party took place that year. Fidel had planned some years before to use it to inaugurate a swing back to small scale private enterprise. But now, he argued to put his own plans on hold, recognizing that it would at that time unleash a process that could deliver Cuba into the hands of the trans-nationals. Cuba would have to survive the immediate crisis before it could confidently establish new internal and external relations.

Fidel railed against the cant about "democracy" that was, and is, the stock-in-trade of the White House:

How can you talk about democracy to a child abandoned in the street? How can you talk about democracy with a hungry person, an illiterate person, an unemployed person, one who has nothing, one to whom no one pays any attention, who nobody respects, who people with money treat like a dog? What democracy can exist in a society of exploiters and exploited?

He had taken to ending his speeches with "Socialism or Death", underscoring his refusal to surrender to what was at that time taken to be the final victory of neo-liberal capitalism. At the congress he fused a sense of emergency with its apparent opposite—unbridled optimism:

Men may die, but examples never die. Men may die, but ideals will never die. And here we are, willing to shed our blood for our ideals! Without honor and dignity, there cannot be life, nor is life worth anything, nor do we want life. So I will change the slogan for this afternoon. Just today, I will not say "Socialist or Death", because there will be socialism whatever the price! I do not say "Homeland or Death", because we shall be able to destroy anyone who wants to take away our homeland!

Still, the collapse of the Soviet Union was a hammer blow to Cuba; it lost nearly $6 billion in trade in 1992 alone. That same year, Yeltsin used U.S. loans to buy sugar from any source except Cuba. In the triumphalist atmosphere of George Bush Sr.'s "New World Order" key Western European states joined the U.S. in endorsing the embargo on Cuba, in defiance of UN General Assembly votes.

A Chinese hand of friendship

Even as Cuba was deserted by its former allies of the Soviet bloc, China began to explore trade opportunities. Within a decade economic relations had blossomed to the point where today China and Venezuela have emerged as Cuba's main economic partners. Chinese companies supplanted many of the European and Canadian companies which helped keep Cuba afloat in the nineties. In addition to supplying a wide range of consumer goods, they became involved in key sectors such as electricity generation and the nickel industry.

China and Viet Nam were our best friends during the incredibly difficult days of the Special Period, when absolutely no one believed that the Cuban Revolution could survive.

Left: **Havana, November 1993**
Chinese leader Jiang Zemin was to visit Cuba for a second time, as President of China, in April 2001.

"Welcome to the USA?" Cuban emigration

When Bill Clinton suspended the rule giving automatic asylum to Cubans entering the U.S. illegally in 1994, he already knew at personal cost that the issue of emigration from the island did not fit neatly into standard anti-Communist rhetoric. He had once been an incidental casualty of a previous standoff with Cuba over the issue. Back in 1980, when Fidel had relaxed restrictions on emigration, the U.S. government dumped 20,000 Cuban immigrants in Fort Chaffee military base in Arkansas. The resulting riot was one of the reasons why Clinton was not re-elected governor of the state that year.

Cuban migration to the U.S. and the response of successive incumbents in the White House are part of the wider migration patterns of Latin America and the Caribbean. These regions have traditionally supplied labor to fill the maw of the U.S. economy, but only when it served the interests of big business. Despite all the verbiage about offering sanctuary from "Communist tyranny" the U.S. has been as concerned to limit the flow of economic migrants from Cuba as it has been to restrict immigration from elsewhere in Latin America.

Right: **Cuban film poster**
The film is called "Viva la República"—"Long live the Republic."

The wrong kind of migrants

The self-interest of the millionaire, ultra-right leaders of the CANF (Cuban American National Foundation) has also been at odds with their "freedom and democracy" dogmatism. For the bulk of Cubans who left the island, certainly in the 1990s, are not cut from anything like the same cloth as the wealthy Díaz-Balart family or other embittered elements of the pre-revolutionary Cuban plutocracy. They are, like their counterparts from Mexico and the rest of Latin America, economic migrants who maintain connections with their homeland, send money back to their relatives, and take the most demeaning jobs in the labor market.

The first migrants from Cuba in the early years after the revolution comprised large numbers of the white middle and upper classes—and they got a red-carpet welcome. When the revolution took a radical turn in the early 1960s, they were the people who provided the core of what would become a ferocious and well-organized opposition to Fidel on the American mainland.

But as early as 1965 Fidel, in seeking to establish a controlled method of emigration, deftly exposed the hypocrisy behind the talk of offering political asylum. In September that year he announced that all those who wished to leave the island would be allowed to do so. There were no direct flights, so he opened the port of Camarioca for Cuban exiles to pick up their relatives by boat. Several thousand Cubans headed for the fishing port and hundreds of boats headed out from Florida.

The U.S. government moved swiftly to open talks with Havana over allowing regular flights. President Johnson was concerned to limit the number of Cubans entering the U.S. even if that meant an agreement with Fidel.

A second "boatlift" took place in 1980. It was a difficult year for Cuba and for Fidel. His great friend Celia Sánchez died that year from lung cancer. There were more than the usual economic difficulties. Diplomatically, Fidel's support for the Soviets caused tensions in the Non-Aligned Movement following the invasion of Afghanistan. The "golden seventies" had come to an end. In April of that year, some Cubans seeking asylum crashed a lorry into the grounds of the Peruvian embassy, killing a Cuban guard.

The Peruvian ambassador said he would not hand over those responsible. Fidel was enraged. He said that if an embassy refused to co-operate in that way, then he could not guarantee the policing of the embassy compound. He then withdrew the guards from the embassy, and over 10,000 Cubans entered the grounds seeking passage.

They ended up not in the U.S., which turned its back on most of them, but in Peru. While mobilizing popular opinion against the emigrants, Fidel also announced, as he had 15 years earlier, that all who wanted to leave would be allowed to do so. Hundreds of boats headed from Florida to the harbor of Mariel. President Carter, allowing a flush of ideological rhetoric to trump the self-interest of U.S. business, said, "Ours is a country of refugees … We'll continue to provide an open heart and open arms to refugees seeking freedom from communist domination."

That rhetoric evaporated in four months. Cuba allowed prisoners to join the emigration. But that was not the main problem for Carter, for whom the "Mariel exodus" proved one of the disasters that marked his last year in the White House. The spectacle of large numbers of Cuban immigrants provided a ready target for xenophobia—what's more, the immigrant-bashing came from the same terrain inhabited by the anti-Fidel right!

For these later migrants were, well, not exactly the kind that would be welcome in the haunts of the Cuban American right wing élite. They were poor, and they were black or mixed race. Worse, though they sought a greater dollar income in the U.S., they usually told waiting reporters how wonderful the welfare system was back home in Cuba. "Their reception in Florida was not as welcoming as they might have hoped," commented British journalist Richard Gott. While the images of people fleeing did not do much for Cuba's international standing, the damage the U.S. did to its own reputation was greater.

Similarly, there was panic in Washington in 1994 over the third big migration from the island, which blew open the ideological barrage against Fidel. The crisis was resolved when Ricardo Alarcón negotiated with the Americans the provision of 20,000 visas annually for Cubans wishing to migrate to the U.S. In return, the Cubans promised to try to limit illegal migration. There were serious attempts—promoted by both Democrat and Republican politicians—during the 1990s to tighten the garrote round Cuba's neck, but the accord on migration spoke volumes about the cynicism of politicians.

Over the decades since the revolution it is estimated that something approaching a million Cubans have left the island. For Fidel, some of those people were very welcome to go. They included the likes of Jorge Más Canosa, who founded the CANF in the 1980s and led it until his death in 1997. Others, though, especially in the early years, were skilled workers and professionals, and their departure damaged Cuba. Still others were simply Latin/Caribbean migrants who were part of the flow of people and counter-flow of dollar earnings that are a familiar feature of life in the shadow of the world's biggest power.

What could *not* be inferred from the migrations was the imminent fall of Fidel. The hard right in the U.S. implicitly acknowledged this at each stage. That's why the years following 1994 were not characterized by the U.S. extending the hand of friendship to the Cuban people. That would be a logical course if Fidel were as unpopular as the CANF proclaimed: a few gestures to the mass of Cubans would surely precipitate his fall. Instead came a renewed campaign to isolate the island. However, a significant section of American business feared losing out to foreign competitors in Cuba. Some sectors backed new U.S. laws which punished non-U.S. companies seeking to do business in Cuba. Others lobbied for a relaxation of the blockade, successfully in the case of the U.S. food multinationals.

Like all U.S. presidents, Bill Clinton pandered to the right-wing Cuban lobby, outflanking Bush Sr. from the right in a Miami fund-raising speech during the 1992 presidential contest. Fidel, however, has been typically generous in his comments about Clinton:

I don't have a bad personal opinion of Clinton. It was the poorest people of the U.S. who elected him. I believe he is a man with good intentions. He wanted to help the unemployed, youth, older people, blacks and Hispanics … But he has not been sufficiently firm in his positions. He has let the mafia-like groups influence him a great deal. This has enabled the far right to exert pressure on him. There was unrest fomented by the right and Clinton came out weakened.

International protests at the U.S. embargo

As the 1990s wore on international support for the U.S. blockade ebbed away. At the U.N. General Assembly in 2000, 166 out of 189 member-states voted alongside Cuba and against the embargo. The only states to vote with the U.S. in positively upholding it were Israel and the ever dependable, and dependent, Marshall Islands. Fidel commissioned expert reports that put the cost to Cuba of the blockade at $67 billion over the first forty years of the Revolution.

One indication of just how isolated the U.S. was in pursuing its vendetta against Cuba is the fact that in the mid-1990s hardened Thatcherites in the British Conservative Party responded positively to those of us who were lobbying for the government to establish stable trade relations with Cuba. David Davis, MP, for example, remarked in the debate:

They intercept everything because the blockade is much more than the banning of buying and selling. The blockade is a tireless hounding of every commercial activity that the country might try to conduct ...

Left: **Matoshinos Conference Center, Oporto, Portugal, October 1998**
Portuguese supporters demonstrating against the U.S. economic blockade of Cuba during the VIII Ibero-American Summit.

CANF and the Cuban-American right

U.S. policy towards Cuba has always reflected American Great Power interests. But it has been given a particular inflection by rich, ultra right Cuban émigrés. Their influence grew considerably in the last decade of the twentieth century, as their dark network of patronage and political blackmail spread out from Miami into the critical nodes of U.S. politics.

One incident in 1996 during Bill Clinton's presidency, which got scant attention during Republican moves to impeach him, indicates the power of the "Cuban-American lobby." According to the report by Kenneth Starr into Clinton's affair with Monica Lewinsky, the president told her on Presidents' Day that year that he "had to put a stop" to their relationship. Lewinsky remembered that at that moment he got a call from someone she named as "Fanuli." The phone call was in fact from Florida sugar magnate Alfonso Fanjul. Clinton dropped everything, as it were, and quickly returned the call, spending a long time on the phone to Fanjul even though the day was a public holiday.

Vice-president Al Gore had announced a plan to levy a small tax on Florida sugar growers in order to pay for the clean up of the Everglades, which were being relentlessly destroyed—not least by pollution from the industrialized production of sugar. The tax was in reality a small cut to the $1.4 billion subsidy Fanjul and the other sugar magnates enjoyed—a subsidy that allowed them to inflate domestic prices and dump mountains of sugar abroad at the expense of poor producing countries such as Cuba. The Fanjul family were major donors to both the Democrats and Republicans. Florida was going to be a key battleground in Clinton's re-election bid. The majority of residents in the state wanted the sugar growers to pay their fair share. But, unsurprisingly, Clinton backed off from cutting the subsidy and the measure fell in Congress after leading Democrats switched sides at the last minute.

The bill that was passed allocated $200 million of public money for the environmental cleanup. It was supported by ostensibly anti big government Republicans such as Senator Bob Dole. He was about to start his run for the presidency. Alfonso Fanjul's brother, José, was part of Dole's all-important fundraising committee. The brothers spread their bets: the Fanjul-owned Flo-Sun Land company donated $50,000 to Clinton's campaign.

By the mid-1990s the influence of wealthy Cuban Americans went way beyond their capacity to wield electoral blocs in the states of Florida and New Jersey. Their role in financing political campaigns gave them disproportionate power in key Congressional committees and meant they could insist on a hard anti-Cuba line from aspiring politicians. The interests of the former masters of Havana were directly represented in the Congress. Chief among the standard bearers was none other than Florida Congressman Lincoln Díaz-Balart, nephew of Fidel's first wife, Mirta. Behind him stood the largesse of the Bacardí rum dynasty and the 55,000-strong Cuban American National Foundation (CANF).

The foundation had been set up in the early 1980s by Jorge Más Canosa. He had left Cuba aged 21 in 1960 and spent the next three decades supporting and funding every plot he could to overthrow Fidel and the revolutionary government. He backed the Bay of Pigs invasion and funded exile groups which often turned to terror tactics. The worst single act of terrorism in the Americas before 9/11 was the bombing of a Cuban airplane on October 6, 1976, on its way home with the national junior fencing team after a successful tournament. The atrocity claimed 73 lives.

There was a mass of evidence that two notorious Cuban exiles and CIA collaborators, Orlando Bosch and Posada Cariles, were responsible. At the time of writing the U.S. government is preventing the extradition of Cariles to Venezuela to face charges (he escaped from prison in Venezuela before being tried for the bombing).

Terror attacks on Cuba did not stop in the 1980s. But Más Canosa, impressed by the success of the American Israel Public Affairs Committee in pressuring politicians to maintain a pro-Israel stance, set up the CANF to do the same for the Cuban American millionaires. He said, "We had to stop the commando raids and concentrate on influencing public opinion and government." For all the cant about Cuban independence, the CANF was the political heir to those sections of the Cuban élite that José Martí had attacked in the nineteenth century for subsuming the liberation struggle against Spain under the demand for annexation by the U.S.

The CANF's nostalgia for the days of U.S. overlordship had a direct, pecuniary motivation as well: the former first families of 1950s Cuba wanted the land and property they had expropriated over generations back in their hands. Their avarice was explicit in the wave of legislation passed in the U.S. in the 1990s designed to tighten the noose around a Cuba that was struggling to recover from the dislocation of the first years of the decade. The Torricelli Act of 1992 and the Helms-Burton Act of 1996 were attempts to extend the strictures against doing business with Cuba that American companies faced to non-U.S. companies.

These measures were also testimony to the breakthrough Cuba had made in recovering from the crisis of the Special Period and forging joint economic ventures with consortia based in Canada, Europe and Latin America. The Helms-Burton Act opened the way to court action in the U.S. against any foreign company that "trafficked in property" that had once belonged to a Cuban or U.S. citizen or U.S. corporation, but which had since been nationalized. It was a naked bid to turn the clock back half a century. Fidel spelled out to the Cuban public and world opinion what it would mean:

"I don't know how they will manage, since even I, who have been traversing our countryside for more than 30 years and participating in road and highway construction programs, can get lost when I go through the province of Havana … Our countryside has been filled with … schools, dams, canals, storehouses, workshops, state-owned enterprises and co-operatives … I do not think there is anyone alive who knows where his large landed estate once was. It is even possible they will find it under a dam … It is impossible for our homeland to turn back."

But the Miami Cuban rich were dusting down their property deeds—or, at any rate, bits of paper that might pass for one—and they were dressing up the attempted land-grab in the lofty phrases of democracy. Objective observers, however, saw a return to the Platt Amendment of 1901, which had stipulated that a notionally independent government in Havana would be constitutionally subservient to Washington. Under the acts of the 1990s, said Cuban leader Ricardo Alarcón, "there would be no Cuban government and no Republic of Cuba. There would be a U.S. council designed by the U.S. president that would look after the Cuban economy." There was widespread opposition from Europe and Canada to the legislation, especially as it extended U.S. jurisdiction to trans-nationals based in other states. The European Union took legislative countermeasures, threatening a trade war with the U.S., but backed off from confrontation at the eleventh hour. But in the U.S. itself, the fanatical anti-Fidel forces felt they could carry public opinion behind them.

Pope John Paul II's visit to Cuba

On January 21, 1998, Pope John Paul II landed in Havana. It was the first ever papal visit to the country. Light-minded commentators in Washington assumed that the anti-Communist Polish pope would trigger the kind of popular unrest that had done for the regime in his native country. But Cuba was not Poland. The Catholic Church had never been as influential on the island. Though early on in the Revolution Fidel had clashed with clerics who had tried to undermine the government, he and the Cuban Communist Party had offered the hand of friendship to the Catholic Church and other religions in 1991. Moreover, the late 1990s were very different from the late 1980s.

The Soviet Union had gone, but neo-liberal globalization was leaving a trail of devastation. Hundreds of millions of people were being thrown backward, fed into the maw of corporate power. In the advanced countries, there were stirrings against the worship of consumerism and greed. War had returned to the European continent (Yugoslavia); it had never left Africa and was about to be unleashed yet again in the Middle East. John Paul II, for all his conservative theology, placed the church firmly on the side of social justice. Fidel, who had been educated in a Jesuit school, rejected the crude anti-religious demagogy that still passes for radicalism in some quarters. A few days before the Pope's visit, he answered a journalist who asked him about his own beliefs.

"These are personal matters about which I do not speak in public. Besides, if I say now that I don't believe I will upset those Cubans who do believe in God; if I answer that I do believe, I will become a preacher for religion that I am not. I respect believers and non-believers; I have respect for any religious conviction. That is the duty of a politician." On his visit, the Pope expressed concern at the tolerance Fidel's government afforded Afro-Cuban religious practices, which were common on the island, and called for greater freedoms for the church and for other associations. A few took these words as encouragement for dissent. But the overall impact of the Pope's visit, and the thrust of what he said, enhanced the reputation of the small island up against the imperialist leviathan to the north. He held the most significant mass of the visit in Revolution Square in Havana, discussing the punitive effects of blind market forces:

"…it is helpful to recall that a modern state cannot make atheism or religion one of its political ordinances. The state, while distancing itself from all extremes of fanaticism or secularism, should encourage a harmonious social climate and suitable legislation which enables every person and every religious group to live its faith freely … On the other hand, some places are witnessing the resurgence of a certain capitalist neo-liberalism which subordinates the human person to blind market forces, and conditions the development of peoples on those forces. From its centers of power, such neo-liberalism often places unbearable burdens upon less favored countries. Hence, at times, unsustainable economic programs are imposed on nations as a condition for further assistance. In the international community, we thus see a small number of countries growing exceedingly rich at the cost of the growing impoverishment of a great number of other countries; as a result the wealthy grow wealthier, while the poor grow ever poorer."

As a footnote to his visit, in his farewell address the Pontiff attacked the four-decade U.S. embargo on Cuba. This was not the message that the CANF and the U.S. right had hoped to hear.

In our day, no nation can live in isolation. The Cuban people therefore cannot be denied the contacts with other people necessary for economic, social and cultural development, especially when the imposed isolation strikes the population indiscriminately, making it ever more difficult for the weakest to enjoy the bare essentials of living.

Pope John Paul II

Right: **Havana International Airport, January 21, 1998**
His Holiness John Paul II being received on his arrival in Cuba.

The story of Elián González

The ultra-right in Miami did not give up its destabilization efforts. In 1999 a five-year old boy, Elián González, was picked up off the coast of Florida when a raft of Cuban migrants capsized. His mother had drowned, and his father, who was still in Cuba, wanted him back.

The CANF drove the campaign to hold him in the U.S. against his father's wishes—the accurate word is kidnap. Elián's great uncle lived in Miami and was associated with hard-line anti-Fidel forces. The CANF swung into action, presenting themselves as the guardians of Elián, his protectors from Fidel's tyranny.

On the boy's sixth birthday, on December 6, he was photographed at his great uncle's home wearing a helmet, wrapped in the Stars and Stripes, surrounded by weapons and striking a martial pose—against Havana.

For six months the Cuban-American right fought against the federal authorities, which went along with all legal precepts in deciding to return the child to his father. Lincoln Díaz-Balart, no doubt embittered by his own clan's battle with Fidel four decades previously over custody of his son Fidelito, played a particularly dishonorable role. Elián wanted to be with his father, but Díaz-Balart took to the airwaves to claim that what was being done was for the boy's own good. He turned up in a blaze of publicity to the house where Elián was being kept and presented him with a Labrador puppy. As one U.S. comment piece put it: "Elián has lost his mother. He needs his father and his grandparents, not a Labrador puppy."

The CANF and its entourage looked mean-spirited and positively vindictive. A *New York Times* columnist called them "an out-of-control banana republic within the American body politic."

José Basulto, founder of "Brothers to the Rescue", then chimed in. It was his hard-line group that, in January 1996, had flown aircraft into Cuban airspace and dropped leaflets onto the streets of Havana calling for the overthrow of Fidel. In response to the outcry about the Cuban Americans' outrageous behavior regarding Elián, he tartly responded that he "couldn't care less what the American public thinks about the Cuban exile community."

In April, Elián was reunited with his father at a Washington airbase. The following month they returned to Cuba. Significantly, 80 percent of Americans and 63 percent of the residents of Miami had told pollsters that they favored the boy's return.

At the time of writing Elián is living in the Cuban seaside town of Cárdenas. A room in the town's small museum has been given over to his story. Elián's father, Juan Miguel, was elected to the National Assembly in 2003, though he still works as a waiter in the Varadero tourist resort just outside Cárdenas. Elián sometimes appears in the front row at public events. He has clearly won the deep affection of the Cuban people and of Fidel.

The real shipwreck of Elian did not take place on the high seas, but when he set foot in America.

Gabriel García Márquez

Right: **Havana, February 2000**
Fidel in conversation with the grandparents of Elián González at the start of one of the many marches demanding Elián's return to Cuba.

Interview with José Pertierra

WASHINGTON D.C., June 2006

José Pertierra is a Washington based immigration lawyer. He arrived in the United States from Cuba as a child with his mother, who was fleeing the tyranny of ... her mother-in-law. He represents the Government of Venezuela in its request for the extradition from the United States of the Cuban born terrorist Posada Carriles, wanted for trial in relation to the sabotage of a Cuban plane in 1976 which resulted in the deaths of all 73 people on board. In the photograph he is with Elián González's father, Juan Miguel, whom he successfully represented in his efforts to have Elián returned to Cuba.

You have met Fidel Castro on several occasions in the course of your professional work. How do you assess him as a man, and as a leader?

It has been said that philosophers interpret the world in various ways, but that the point is to change it. Fidel has dedicated his life to change. He is a visionary who strives to change things in order to try and improve the lot of the poor people of this earth. From Africa's shanty towns to the forgotten slums of Latin America, Cuba's physicians and teachers dedicate their lives to improving the lives of their brothers and sisters overseas. Fidel's constant reminder that a better world is possible gives fuel to those who strive along with him to change society.

Throughout the past half century of tumultuous change Cuba has managed to create and defend an independent national state, in the face of constant U.S. hostility. How do you assess Fidel Castro's role in this?

Wherever United States Presidents go in their minds, they will find Fidel on his way back. He knows what U.S. politicians will do before they themselves know. This singular ability to outwit Washington is the prime reason why the Cuban revolution has been able to survive over four decades of state sponsored terrorism against it, and a brutal blockade by the U.S. government designed to starve the Cuban people into submission.

Fidel seems to have taken on a brand new lease of life since his allies Hugo Chávez, in Venezuela, and Evo Morales, in Bolivia, have come to power. How important is his role in the reshaping of a more independent Latin America?

Presidents Chávez and Morales are products of their own societies. They have found in the Cuban revolution and in Fidel a source of inspiration, and an economic and political ally in the face of U.S. hostility. The U.S.-inspired attempted coup against President Chávez in 2002 made it abundantly clear that Washington intends to try and depose the Bolivarian revolution by any means necessary. President Morales has barely been able to enjoy a political honeymoon and already we are receiving reports of U.S. military and political maneuvers against his government.

The Cuban revolution is an example of independence, survival and sovereignty in a continent that for far too long has been nothing more than the backyard of the United States. A united Latin America standing tall and independent from U.S. control was the dream of

Simon Bolívar, José Martí, and Ernesto Guevara. Their dream is now been carried forth by Hugo Chávez, Fidel Castro and Evo Morales.

What connection do you see between Fidel's approach to Latin America today and in the sixties, when he and Che Guevara backed guerrilla struggles against U.S. puppet regimes?

Fidel recognizes that times have changed. The battle for the future of Latin America is no longer fought with the barrel of the gun. It is a battle of ideas for the hearts and minds of the new generation of Latinos. Already, this battle of ideas is bearing fruits, as progressive governments are assuming power throughout Latin America. The ability to change with the times is what distinguishes revolutionaries from mere metaphysicians.

Why won't the U.S. government negotiate with Fidel? Is it because it is in thrall to the political right wing of the Cuban American community, or because it does not believe it could win the concessions it wants while Fidel is in power?

The Cuban American community does not have the power in the U.S. that it thinks it has. Instead, hardliners in the U.S. government have found in them a natural ally in the holy war against Communism that Washington has been fighting for decades. Indeed, elements within the U.S. government and its intelligence agencies have used Cuban Americans militarily, as well as politically, to wage its holy war. The dirty wars of Latin America were fought with Cuban American foot soldiers. From Chile to Buenos Aires, Caracas, and even Washington, D.C. the bloody claws of the Condor were Cuban American. If and when the U.S. government decides it is in its interests to negotiate with the Cuban Revolution, it will do so no matter what the Miami Cubans do or say. Until then, Miami Cubans are useful to Washington because there is a coincidence of interests between them.

Presumably the U.S. oil companies will win a modification of the embargo to permit them to make joint ventures with the Cuban government for deep sea exploration in the Florida straits—just as the U.S. food corporations did some years ago. Will this be the beginning of the end of the embargo and, if so, how will the U.S. government come to terms with Fidel then?

President Calvin Coolidge said in the 1920s that "the business of America is business." Consistent with that maxim, the wedge that will punch a hole in the U.S. blockade against Cuba will be business. Once important U.S. corporations see in Cuba a place where lots of money can be made, then the wishes of the Miami Cubans will be brushed aside by Washington.

This country is really run by multinationals, and it will be they who finally will end the blockade. Offshore oil in Cuba may be the catalyst for this change. Time will tell. A lot depends on what the oil explorations off of Cuba's coasts will tell us in the next few months and years.

Luis Posada Carriles, the Cuban émigré who has carried out terrorist operations for the CIA against Cuba since the 1960s, and in Central America during the Iran-Contra years of the eighties, is currently being held in a Texas jail on trumped up immigration charges. The Venezuelan government, which you represent, wants him extradited to face trial for the sabotage of a Cuban plane in 1976. Carriles, quite literally, seems to know where many bodies are buried and President

Bush seems terrified of him. What potential does this case have for unraveling the aggressive approach that the U.S. government has pursued towards Cuba, Venezuela and other countries of Latin America?

Posada Carriles knows where the skeletons are hidden. He is a professional intelligence operative who has been the key player in U.S. operations against Cuba since 1961. From the Bay of Pigs operation in 1961, in which he participated, to his attempt in 2000 to blow up an auditorium full of students at the University of Panamá where President Castro was to speak, Posada Carriles has a long and bloody résumé of terror.

He has never been, however, a loose cannon. Posada has always been a loyal soldier in Washington's holy war against Communism. The U.S. had advance knowledge of the plans to down the passenger plane in 1976 that killed 73 people (including a pregnant woman and a nine year old girl). CIA cables that have been declassified and are now on the web tell us that three months before the bombing of the plane, the CIA informed Washington that Posada's Cuban exile group planned to carry out an attack on a Cuban passenger plane.

A month before the bombing, Posada himself was overheard by the CIA to say that a Cuban passenger plane would be hit. Washington did nothing about it. They neither called off Posada, nor informed Cuban authorities, nor alerted the airports to beef up their security to try and avert the strike.

Sometimes silence says more than words. After his arrest in Caracas for 73 counts of first degree murder in relation to the bombing of the plane, Posada was able to escape with at least $50,000 from a prominent Cuban American exile organization in Miami. He immediately was flown to San Salvador to work alongside Colonel

Oliver North in the operation later known as the Iran-Contra scandal.

After the dismantling by Congress of the illegal arms to the Contras operation, Posada turned up in Guatemala, Honduras, and El Salvador as a special consultant to Central American death squads. His own lawyer is now arguing that Posada should be naturalized as a U.S. citizen because of services he performed for the U.S. government during times of "hostilities abroad."

Moreover, Posada is now threatening to call as witnesses on his behalf U.S. government officials such as Colonel North and perhaps even President Bush Sr., who was the head of the CIA in 1976 when the downing of the plane occurred, and Vice-President of the United States during Iran-Contra.

Venezuela wants Posada tried for 73 counts of first degree murder in relation to the downing of the plane. The extradition treaties give the U.S. no legal option other than either extraditing him to Venezuela or prosecuting him in the U.S. for murder. Much as the U.S. would like for the Posada litigation to go away (and perhaps Posada himself), the case will not go away, and Venezuela will not rest until this terrorist is brought to justice.

Next page: **A wall in Cuba, May 2006**
One of many murals around the country calling for the return of the Five Heroes, the Cubans imprisoned in the United States for uncovering terrorist plots by Miami based Cuban émigré groups.

"Bernardo Rdguez."
¡Con la guardia en alto!
CDR
Tony, Fernando y Ramón,
Por eso cada nación
la lucha tenaz inicia
no practica la Justicia.
AUTOR:
Everildo Pérez.

Above: **Havana, May 2002**

Fidel greeting former U.S. president Jimmy Carter.

Jimmy Carter: a historic visit

In May 2002 Nobel prizewinner and former U.S. president Jimmy Carter toured Cuba for several days. The last U.S. president to visit the island had been Calvin Coolidge in 1928. Carter took the opportunity to lecture the Cubans about human rights, but he acknowledged that the death penalty was more readily applied in the U.S. than in Cuba, and the main thrust of his speeches was for lifting the embargo.

George W. Bush's administration, however, was moving in the opposite direction, seizing on 9/11 to bracket Cuba with other members of the "Axis of Evil." While Carter was still in Havana, the U.S. State Department spread the false rumor that Fidel was developing biological weapons.

> It is time for us to change our relationship ... Because the United States is the most powerful nation, we should take the first step.

former U.S. president Jimmy Carter, May 2002

We have come through!

Much of the restructuring that had been put on hold in the wake of the Soviet collapse had been quietly implemented, and the Cuban leadership especially sought to engage with young people. It was the beginning of the cultural explosion that brought Cuba to the attention of a wider and new generation internationally. The economy seemed at last to have bottomed out.

At home and abroad Fidel came across as the model of principled flexibility. "We are surrounded by capitalists on all sides," he told the Cuban people. "We cannot ignore capitalism, any more than we can ignore the sea around us." Cuba's response was to promote the rapid development of the tourism industry, which by the end of the decade was bringing in hundreds of thousands of visitors and much needed foreign earnings. Biotechnology at the high-value end of world trade was another earner, though its potential remained curtailed by the U.S. blockade.

Cuba no longer seemed so isolated. Visits by Fidel abroad often brought new modes of understanding with other world leaders. The U.S.'s obsessive boycott of Fidel's Cuba now began to look like the anachronism. And, as the new millennium dawned, a global sentiment against corporate hegemony was turning into a movement which, three decades after the overthrow of Allende, was to hoist up a new generation of left leaders in Latin America.

Right: **Conference Center, Havana, 2004**
Fidel with Raúl Castro during a session of the National Assembly of People's Power.

Cuban science and biotechnology

From the beginning, Fidel had stated that "Cuba's future must, by necessity, be a future of scientists."

In the early years of the Revolution two scientific centers were established: an institute for research into sugarcane derivatives and a national center for scientific research. These centers were the nuclei for creating numerous other scientific institutions. They were concerned with animal and plant health, biological research, genetic engineering and biotechnology, immunoassay, molecular immunology, pharmaceutical chemistry, the rearing of laboratory animals, neurological restoration, neurosciences and bioproducts.

By 1980 there were 35 university centers (from six in 1958), which matriculated 240,000 students in 1990. Thousands of these students were sent abroad for advanced scientific training, mainly in the Soviet Union, the GDR and Czechoslovakia. In 1997 more than 30,000 people were employed in some two hundred institutions, eleven thousand of them professionals and nine thousand of them technicians.

In 1980 Fidel heard about experimental work with interferons for the treatment of cancer at the M. D. Anderson Cancer Center at the University of Texas, and made the decision to invest in this new biotechnology. This was at the time of the "Carter thaw," when the U.S. and Cuba opened diplomatic "interest sections" in each other's countries and travel was temporarily eased. Cuban scientists were sent to study at M. D. Anderson, and at the Helsinki laboratory of Kari Cantell.

The Center for Biological Research was founded for the production and cloning of interferons and for research in molecular biology and biotechnology in general. The Center for Genetic

Engineering and Biotechnology was opened in 1986, and some $100 million invested in pharmaceuticals, immunodiagnostics, vaccines and animal, plant and industrial biotechnology. This was to rise to over $1 billion over the following two decades.

The objective was to meet Cuba's domestic needs and develop low cost products that could be traded in the Third World. Progress slowed when Cuba faced a desperate economic situation after the collapse of the Soviet Union, but picked up again as the economy improved in the second half of the nineties.

Cuba has succeeded in making alliances with several foreign companies to take pharmaceutical products to registration and into the international marketplace. The most notable was with SmithKline Beecham to develop Cuba's meningitis B vaccine, which required a decision from the U.S. Treasury Department to make an exception to the U.S. embargo legislation. Other joint ventures have been established with companies from Canada, Iran and India, for products such as a hepatitis B vaccine, anti-cancer interferons and streptokinase for treating cardiac arrest.

Cuba is now generating a substantial income from exporting biotech products to other Third World countries. These are products that in many cases would not be developed by multinational pharmaceutical companies, because the development costs in high wage western countries would be too high for them to be profitable.

Next page: **Teatro Karl Marx, Havana, 2005**
Fidel and Venezuelan president Hugo Chávez presenting degree certificates to the first students to graduate from Cuba's Latin American School of Medicine.

Nurturing champions

Cuba has had remarkable success in sports. In 1992 it came fifth in the Barcelona Olympics, an extraordinary achievement for a nation of eleven million.

Cuba's success, as in much else, has been the result of the careful nurturing of talent. One of Cuba's earliest champions was Teófilo Stevenson, who was brought from Santiago de Cuba to a sports academy in Havana at the age of twelve and went on to win the Olympic heavyweight boxing title three times. Muhammad Ali, on one of his visits to Cuba, said that Stevenson is the one boxer who could have beaten him at his peak.

Left: **Havana, 2005**
Fidel with a group of Cuban Olympic medallists. Second from left is the boxer Teófilo Stevenson. Fourth from left is Ana Fidelia Quirot, a top world 800 meter runner throughout the nineties, who is now a member of Cuba's National Assembly. Third from left is Diego Maradonna, the Argentine soccer genius who lives in Cuba following successful drug rehabilitation.

chapter 8
A truly Latin revolutionary

Fidel and the future

Among historians, the period 1914 to 1989 is sometimes known as the short 20th century. By that yardstick, the succeeding 21st century, with its supposed final triumph of U.S.-led capitalist globalization, has turned out to be, well, Lilliputian in stature.

Barely had the victory of neo-liberalism been declared, when it came under sustained critique and then global assault by a new upsurge of radical left activism heralded by the Seattle protests in 1999 and prefigured by the Zapatista uprising in Chiapas, Mexico, in 1994. The events of the next few years left Fidel, according to all who knew him, "seeming young again." What seemed tired and anachronistic, by contrast, was the grim orthodoxy pumped out from Washington, London, and faceless, unaccountable institutions such as the International Monetary Fund and World Bank. Nowhere was their life-denying doctrine more challenged than in Latin America.

As Fidel approached his 80th birthday in August 2006, neither he nor Cuba faced the isolation they had endured a decade and a half earlier. A new generation of left leaders had begun to emerge across Latin America. Venezuela's President Hugo Chávez had not been born when Fidel made his "History will Absolve me" speech in the wake of the Moncada assault in 1953. Evo Morales, the left wing president of Bolivia, was born 10 months after the victorious rebels entered Havana on New Year's Day 1959.

In seeking the tightest possible bonds of friendship with Fidel and Cuba, Chávez and Morales have unerringly anticipated the

Previous page: **Fidel, Havana, May 2006**
Speaking on the ALBA trade agreement with Cuba, Venezuela and Bolivia

judgment of history which Fidel had placed himself before over half a century previously.

They share the inspiration Fidel took from the great Latin American heroes Simón Bolívar and José Martí. So, for Hugo Chávez it was not enough to use the wealth of Venezuela's oil industry to benefit the country's poor, for the first time in its history. It also meant supplying Cuba with cheap oil in return for sorely needed Cuban health and education expertise. It meant funding for Cuba to train many thousands of medical students from around the world to be sent into the global South. Likewise, the decision by Evo Morales to nationalize Bolivia's natural gas fields not only provided the wherewithal for a program of reforms, it also raised the continental banner of independence from Washington and the multinationals.

The announcement that Chávez and Morales were going to attend the Non-Aligned Movement conference in Havana in September 2006 brought back images of the movement's heyday in the 1970s. Also at the summit were to be representatives of Hamas, which had won the Palestinian Authority elections, and Iran's President Mahmoud Ahmadinejad.

This meeting of leaders, whom the neo-conservatives have placed on their ever expanding "Axis of Evil," betrayed the hollowness of George Bush's boasting about "mission accomplished" in May 2003 following the fall of Baghdad. Far from Iraq having achieved the "demonstration effect" of showcasing, and thus terrorizing, the world with U.S. power, the grinding war and occupation have demonstrated its limits.

Meanwhile, in what the U.S. has long considered its own "backyard" of Latin America, Fidel, Hugo and Evo have responded to Bush by declaring themselves the "Axis of Good."

The wave of protest 30 years ago ... was somewhat isolated. The current wave of protest is widespread; it engulfs all of Latin America.

Left: **Revolution Square, Havana, May 2006**
Fidel with Venezuelan president Hugo Chávez and Bolivian president Evo Morales, holding the flags of their three countries. They have declared themselves the "Axis of Good."

A positive force for good

Ever alert to the movement of world politics, Fidel had recognized that the U.S. disaster in Iraq would give Latin American countries greater room to maneuver in relation to their overbearing northern neighbor. The developing revolt against neo-liberalism has prised open further space for progressive forces across the globe. That is why Fidel would get a joyous reaction from tens of thousands of well-wishers on the streets of any world city he visited. Wherever Bush goes, he requires protection from the people in the street because, as with Macbeth, "those he commands move only in command, nothing in love."

Cuba's health system is on a par with northern Europe's; in the U.S., 40 million people have no health insurance. Life expectancy is higher and infant mortality lower in Havana than in Washington, D.C. As the Cuban poster puts it, "100 million children under the age of 13 are at work rather than school—not one of them in Cuba."

In a world where 16,000 children a day die from hunger, and where money is funneled from people in the poorest countries to the bankers in the richest—as it was when Fidel highlighted the issue of Third World debt in 1979—there's no mystery why Cuba and its leader should stand so tall on the world stage. An island that was once the bordello of the Caribbean is now the global medical resource of tens of millions. This book has been the story of what Fidel achieved after he set off in Martí's footsteps. It is fitting, therefore, that Martí's words provide its coda:

Men of action, above all those whose actions are guided by love, live forever. Other famous men, those of much talk and few deeds, soon evaporate. Action is the dignity of greatness.

José Martí

Interview with Dr. Wayne S. Smith

WASHINGTON, D.C., June 2006

Dr. Wayne S. Smith was assigned to the American Embassy in Havana as a young diplomat from July of 1958, before Castro marched into Havana, until the U.S. broke diplomatic relations in January of 1961. He was with the first group of American diplomats back into Havana, in April of 1977, to conduct negotiations with the Cubans as part of the Carter administration's efforts to improve relations.

Wayne Smith was named Chief of Mission of the U.S. Interests Section in July of 1979. Efforts to improve relations pretty well ended with the election of Ronald Reagan in 1980, and in 1982, because of his profound disagreements with Reagan's policies, Smith asked to be removed from the post and given a job unrelated to policy until such time as he could take early retirement, then several months away.

In September of 1982, Smith joined the Carnegie Endowment for International Policy and there held his first press conference, at which he publicly took issue with the new administration's policies toward Cuba and Central America. Since then, he has campaigned tirelessly against the absurdity and sterility of the U.S. economic and political blockade of Cuba.

You have had the opportunity, practically unique for an American, to observe Fidel Castro at close quarters since his government first came to power nearly fifty years ago. How did you assess him at the time?

As an extraordinarily formidable opponent. Indeed, he seemed to be the kind of leader who came along only rarely in the life of any nation. It very quickly became apparent that his objectives were antithetical to those of the U.S. He wanted not only to free Cuba completely of U.S. political and economic domination, but also to create a great new Latin American revolutionary block, with himself as the spiritual leader. As the U.S. reaction to this became increasingly threatening, Castro almost inevitably turned to the Soviet Union for support, or, better put, for a shield against U.S. power. That is to say, he was not a Communist when he first came to power. He became one, and turned Cuba into a socialist state, for reasons of strategic defense.

And how has your assessment changed over the years?

My assessment of him has not changed. In my eyes, he remains an extraordinary leader—as demonstrated by the fact that almost fifty years later, and despite all-out U.S. efforts to get rid of him, he remains at the helm in Cuba. And not only that, at the helm of a Cuba that has survived the collapse of the Soviet Union and is moving into a vastly changed situation in Latin America. His role, however, has certainly changed. The Cold War is over and there is really no objective reason at all that the United States could not now work out a normal relationship with Cuba. Cuba demonstrated some years back that it was prepared for that. Castro need no longer be considered a foe, or adversary. The Bush administration, however, rejects that idea and instead has actually moved to an increasingly threatening posture toward Cuba. This will achieve nothing. On the contrary, for the U.S. it is a lose-lose policy.

How do you see his political contribution, to his own country and to other countries, especially in the Third World?

Castro has demonstrated that a small Third World country, even one in Latin America, can achieve and maintain its independence—and an independent policy—in the face of threats and pressures from the most powerful nation in the world. In part as the result of his stubbornness and commitment to a vision, Latin America is now moving perceptibly in his direction, i.e., toward the left. And other Third World states look at the Cuban example and say "if he can do it, so can we."

To quote the title of one of your books, Cuba and the United States have for half a century been "the closest of enemies." Looking back, do you think it was inevitable that Cuba left the U.S. political and economic orbit? Was it perhaps even necessary if Cuba was to establish its independence?

Yes, of course, it was necessary precisely in order to establish its independence. Castro could not possibly have played the role of "U.S. pawn." And yet, as of 1959, the U.S. really expected that any Cuban leader would play exactly that role.

Do you think it could be possible for the two countries to establish normal relations in the not too distant future, even while Fidel is still in the government?

There is no objective reason that the two could not enjoy normal, even cordial, relations. The Cold War is over. Cuba poses no threat whatever to the U.S. The first thing the U.S. should do is lift travel controls, reduce tensions and begin a dialogue to discuss our disagreements. Soon after that, we should begin to lift our trade embargo. We would of course like to see Cuba respond to the relaxation of tensions by easing internal controls.

With the turn away from neoliberal policies throughout Latin America and the formation of what Fidel has taken to calling the Axis of Good centered on Havana-Caracas-La Paz, what role do you see for Fidel Castro? Could we really be on the verge of a second and definitive independence for Latin America, which takes its inspiration from Bolívar and Martí, Che and Fidel?

Well, not necessarily from Che and Fidel. I think Latin America is indeed moving toward a more nationalist, independent model, and one that will no longer follow along in the wake of the United States. On the contrary, thanks to the Bush administration, the standing of the U.S. in the hemisphere has sunk to an all-time low. Who wants to follow Bush? Even so, there are nations, such as Brazil and Chile, which will want to maintain economic ties with the U.S. and will not look to Cuba, or to Venezuela, as their models.

Interview with Alice Walker
CALIFORNIA, U.S.A., June 2006

One of the foremost contemporary American writers, Alice Walker is an internationally admired poet, essayist and novelist. She received the Pulitzer Prize and National Book Award in 1983 for her novel *The Color Purple* (one of 14 novels and short-story collections) and has won numerous literary awards. She was active in the Civil Rights Movement of the 1960s, and is still an involved political activist. She has long advocated ending the embargo against Cuba.

You went to Cuba for the first time in 1978. What were your impressions of the relations between Cubans of different ethnic ancestries?

I went to Cuba in 1978 and there was of course lingering racist behavior and attitudes, which my group of cultural workers—artists, musicians, dancers—pointed out. The Cubans had a good understanding of how hard it is to change ingrained notions of superiority but assured us they were dedicated to doing so. They pointed out that racism itself had been made illegal in Cuba. This was a profound and novel idea that I wished to import to my home state of Georgia, USA. And the rest of North America as well. I had by then toiled long years in Mississippi beside my Civil Rights lawyer husband and watched the slow, sometimes life-threatening process of dismantling racist institutions case by case. There was no comparison between the racism of Mississippi and that of Cuba. Or the response to it. Mississippi was by far the more dangerous place to be.

Fidel has always reached out to the "wretched of the earth," whether poor whites or blacks, the peoples of south-east Asia at the time of the Vietnam War, the peoples of Africa, the indigenous peoples of the Americas. What is your impression of Fidel and what he has done for Cuban society?

It is always apparent to me that Fidel is a deeply religious man. In the Gandhian sense: "I call that man religious who understands the suffering of others." More than any other leader of our time, or of the last century, Fidel has made it his business to understand exactly why people are poor, in whatever country they are in; why they are at war or at peace; why they are suffering. He has a fine, large intellect, which he uses to comprehend and defend the wretched of the earth. And what is most admirable about him, in my opinion, is that he has never once abandoned his scrutiny of the material conditions of the world in an effort to find solutions to the horrible inequities that exist.

He thinks about the same things I do: infant mortality rates, how many calories it takes for a child to do well in school; what is the best way to develop a society in which people feel connected and not alienated. When I am in Cuba I feel safe. Once I was vacationing in Jamaica with my daughter and she was in a motorcycle accident that broke her foot. On the whole side of the Island we could not find one doctor, only a couple of nurse practitioners who had only kindness and a bandage to offer us. In Cuba, even during the periods of almost no food or medical supplies I know my daughter's foot would have been looked after by a doctor, and moreover, a doctor who lived nearby. The Cuban people take such things for granted. They take a lot of things for granted. Free education, health care, low housing costs, their leader's obvious love of them. His pride in their endurance, stamina, compassion for the beleaguered of the world, their innumerable accomplishments.

I have never felt affection, as an American, from a national leader in the United States. When there has been a semblance of genuine as opposed to photo-op caring it has been partisan. And therefore painful. There has been no substantive and sustained attempt to deal with the underlying foundation of genocide and enslavement that created North America's wealth, still in the hands mostly of white families. Yes, I know Oprah has a billion dollars that she uses very well, but this does not mean capitalism, rooted in Indian killing and African enslavement and torture and murder, works.

Cubans, generally, I have found, are intelligent, compassionate people who are curious about Life. Partly because their leaders are. They hold a vision of what is possible different from that most North Americans possess. That is because they are taught more of what is happening on the planet and why. Global warming, for instance, which is only now becoming a hot (so to speak) topic in the U.S., has been in the consciousness of Cubans for years. That is why, when a hurricane struck Havana some years ago the entire city was evacuated before it arrived. Think of the confusion of the U.S. government during hurricane Katrina in New Orleans. It is enough to make us weep. And we will weep, because more of that: confusion, denial, incompetence, is surely in our future.

I was not surprised when Fidel and the Cuban government offered to send supplies and doctors to New Orleans—this is behavior I expect of Cubans after all these years watching them respond to the disasters of the world. And I was ashamed when their generosity was refused, by my childish government, as so many of my people suffered miserably in alligator and snake infested water, and many of them died. This disregard for the black poor, like the disenfranchisement of black people during the last two elections, we can never forget. It is a permanent bruise to the heart.

In the early years of the Cuban Revolution Fidel made contact with many prominent black Americans, such as Angela Davis, Malcolm X, Harry Belafonte, and later with people such as Jesse Jackson and Muhammad Ali. How is Fidel viewed by black Americans today?

I only know a couple of hundred black Americans well enough to guess what they might think about anything. In the world, however, one senses there is a deep respect for Fidel. It is based on the fact that he has stood his ground. That my country's attempts to shut him up and to assassinate him have failed. I have written elsewhere that he is like a lone redwood tree in a forest that's been clear-cut. It is painful to imagine what might have been our current situation if Patrice Lumumba had survived, and Che, and Martin Luther King, Jr. and the long list of names most of us will never be able to connect to each other, but which are connected by their resistance to the terrorism and tyranny of the United States.

In an interview you once remarked that you had heard that Fidel could not sing and he could not dance, so it was just as well he had all those other good qualities. What do you consider his finest qualities?

I have had the pleasure of meeting (with a group of people) with Fidel twice. It's true he talks a lot, and it is incredibly interesting because he enjoys explaining his information. He is a natural teacher. And he has a robust sense of humor. I realize many people, encountering such a force, would immediately think of him as a dictator. But it's different when someone talks a lot and it's about sending doctors around the globe to serve the poor; or it's about why so many young men are suffering from a mysterious eye disease (this was the topic at one of the meetings) or about the exploitation by the United States and Europe over centuries. His grasp of world realities is so profound that he has not one iota of the nervousness that most so-called white leaders display in the presence of alert people of color. This is delightful. But let's linger a moment on the singing and dancing. These are profoundly important to the human spirit, and because Fidel's is a singing and dancing intellect.

I wanted him to embody dance and song in himself. For his own enjoyment. Che was likewise without this embodied solace. Because I love these men, honor what they have accomplished, realize they have dedicated their lives to the alleviation of misery, I want them to have this medicine which I so frequently use. And there is also a part of me that says: you're Cuban, damn it! And before that, Spanish. What about that soulful music you had in Spain, and Flamenco! And then of course I remember Catholicism and its heavy suppressions of the life force. In Fidel this passion is expressed in his priestly dedication to revolution.

Fidel is eighty. It is perhaps selfish of me, but I wish he could retire to the countryside or seashore and enjoy a lengthy period of silence. It would be wonderful for him. And that there might be small children brought by to play with him for a couple of hours each week. I would want him to have a cat that falls asleep on his chest. And if there's a wife, as there must be since there are children, that they hold hands day in, day out. And fall asleep together in the hammock. Enough of leaders being used up, becoming, as Fidel was quoted as saying "the slave of the Revolution." The world is indescribably beautiful. One day of truly witnessing it is enough to revitalize the heart; stilling many worries about the outcomes of the future. I would wish many such days for Fidel.

Happy birthday, Fidel.
  May you be happy.
  May you be peaceful.
  May you be joyful.
May you have health and ease
Of Being
  May you smile again
  from inside your
  fierce spirit.
May you discover naps and cats and
Small children
Who will be charmed
and mystified
By
Your beard.

May you hear us
In our millions
Say to you

As we used to say
In the little country church
Where I am from
"Well done." Good and Faithful
Servant
Well done."
Fidel. Faithful.
You have had the success that
Eludes
So many:
You have lived up to your name.

Photo Credits

Quotation Credits

CHAPTER 1

p17 Speech at the University of Havana, September 4, 1995, in Deborah Shnookal and Pedro Álvarez Tabío (eds), *Fidel: my early years*, Ocean Press, 2005, p85

p20 Eugenio Suárez Pérez and Acela A. Caner Román (eds), *Fidel Castro: Birán to Cinco Palmas*, Editorial José Martí, 2002, p16

p23 Ignacio Ramonet, *Cien Horas con Fidel*, Havana, April 2006, p106

p28 Fidel Castro Archive

p29 Claudia Furiati, *Fidel Castro: La historia me absolverá*, Plaza Janés, 2003, p91

p31 Ramonet, op cit, p92

p39 Furiati, op cit, p54

p40 Suárez Pérez and Caner Román, op cit, p15

CHAPTER 2

p57 Ramonet, op cit, pp124-5

p61 Shnookal and Álvarez Tabío, op cit, p16

p62 Shnookal and Álvarez Tabío, op cit, p89

p67 Ramonet, op cit, p116

p70 Tad Szulc, *Fidel Castro: a critical portrait*, 1986, p288

p80 Marta Harnecker, *From Moncada to Victory*, 1987, p48

p87 Leycester Coltman, *The Real Fidel Castro*, 2003, p79

p92 Coltman, op cit, p91

p100 Furiati, op cit, pp201–2

CHAPTER 3

p113 Quoted in Volker Skierka, *Fidel Castro: a biography*, 2004, p39

p116 Ramonet, op cit, p178

p123 Quoted from memory by Fidel Castro, in Ramonet, op cit, p40

p126 *Face to Face with Fidel Castro: a conversation with Tomás Borge*, Ocean Press, 1993, p156

p132 Suárez Pérez and Caner Román, op cit, p282

p134 Quoted in Richard Gott, *Cuba: a new history*, 2004, p89

p138 Pedro Álvarez Tabío, *Celia: ensayo para una biografía*, Oficina de Publicaciones del Consejo de Estado, Havana, 2004, p230

p140 Szulc, op cit, p395

p152 Álvarez Tabío, op cit, p265

p151 Eugenio Suárez Pérez and Acela A. Caner Román (eds), *Fidel Castro: De*

Cinco Palmas a La Habana, Ediciones Verde Olivo, Havana, 1998, p47

p147 *New York Times*, February 24, 1957

p148 Ibid

p163 Furiati, op cit, p163

p175 *Un Encuentro con Fidel: entrevista realizada por Gianni Miná*, Oficina de Publicaciones del Consejo de Estado, Havana, 1988, p175

p176 Eugenio Suárez Pérez and Acela A. Caner Román (eds), *Fidel Castro: De Cinco Palmas a La Habana*, Ediciones Verde Olivo, Havana, 1998, p356

p185 *Front Page Challenge*, broadcast on CBS, January 13, 1959

p186 *USA Today*, January 19, 2006

CHAPTER 4

p191 Ramonet, op cit, p245

p194 Coltman, op cit, p157

p209 Coltman, op cit, p175

p210 Furiati, op cit, p395

p213 *Fidel Castro: Nothing can stop the course of history*, interview with Jeffrey M. Elliot and Mervyn M. Dymally, Pathfinder Press, 1986, p184

p217 Ernest Hemingway, letter to a friend, 1960

p228 Ramonet, op cit, p259

p233 Ramonet, op cit, p257

p235, Szulc, op cit, pp559-60

p238 Interview in *LOOK*, September 15, 1959

p239 Gott, op cit, p180

CHAPTER 5

p254 Lawrence Chand and Peter Kornbluh (eds), *The Cuban Missile Crisis*, 1998, p356

p256 Coltman, op cit, p205

p257 Coltman, op cit, p206

p278 Quoted in Skierka, op cit, p160

p279 Coltman, op cit, p214

p287 *Tricontinental* magazine, Havana, April 16, 1967

CHAPTER 6

p292 Robert E. Quirk, *Fidel Castro*, 1995, p635

p293 Szulc, op cit, p622

p296 Quirk, op cit, pp698–9

p299 Quoted in Skierka, op cit, p202

p300 Quirk, op cit, p690

p308 *Granma Weekly Review*, January 4, 1976 and 24 November 1974
p311 Various reports, December 5, 1972
p312 Shnookal and Álvarez Tabío, op cit, p36
p317 Quirk, op cit, p736
pp326–7 Coltman, op cit, pp245–6
p331 http://en.wikiquote.org/wiki/Fidel_Castro
p332 http://en.wikiquote.org/wiki/Barbara_Walters
p339 Reuters, September 30, 2005

CHAPTER 7
p356 Coltman, op cit, pp279–280
p357 Coltman, op cit, p281
p359 Speech to National Assembly of People's Power, Havana, March 6, 2003
p374 Quoted in Skierka, op cit, p351
p378 *New York Times*, March 30, 2000

CHAPTER 8
p403 *Clarín* newspaper, Buenos Aires, Argentina, May 26, 2003
p405 http://www.brainyquote.com/quotes/quotes/j/josemarti225395.html

Bibliography

There is an vast literature about Fidel Castro and the Cuban Revolution, and there are many good books about Cuba's history.

An excellent general account is Richard Gott's *Cuba: a new history* (2004). Louis Pérez, Jr., has written many fine books on aspects of Cuban history, including *Cuba: between reform and revolution* (1995) and *On becoming Cuban: identity, nationality and culture* (1999). An excellent introduction to history, culture and politics in Cuba is *The Cuba Reader* (2003), edited by Aviva Chomsky, Barry Carr and Pamela Maria Smorkaloff.

Claudia Furiati wrote a detailed and intimate biography of Fidel entitled *Fidel Castro: la historia me absolverá* (2003), which benefits from interviews made in Cuba with a large number of family and comrades of Fidel, and Fidel himself. Another recent, and also in many ways intimate, biography is Leycester Coltman's *The Real Fidel Castro* (2003), by a former British ambassador to Cuba.

As this book was nearing completion there appeared Ignacio Ramonet's compilation of his conversations with Fidel over two and a half years. In Cuba this is published as *Cien horas con Fidel* (April 2006) and in Spain as *Fidel Castro: biografía a dos voces*. It will shortly be available in most languages and is an invaluable source on Fidel's thoughts on a vast range of topics. Only five previous conversations with Fidel have been published in book form—two with Gianni Miná, one with Frei Betto, one with Tomás Borge and one with Jeffrey M. Elliot and Mervyn M. Dymally.

For those who wish to read more about Che Guevara, I recommend the excellent *Che Handbook* (2003) by Hilda Barrio and Gareth Jenkins, in the same series as the present Handbook.

Other works consulted

Tomás Diez Acosta, *October 1962: the missile crisis as seen from Cuba* (2002)

Sebastian Balfour, *Castro* (1990)

Peter Bourne, *Castro* (1986)

Fidel Castro, *Fidel: my early years* (2005)

Carlos Franqui, *Fidel* (1980)

Marta Harnecker, *From Moncada to Victory* (1987)

H.L. Matthews, *Castro: a political biography* (1969)

Robert E. Quirk, *Fidel Castro* (1995)

Volker Skierka, *Fidel Castro: a biography* (2004)

Tad Szulc, *Fidel: a critical portrait* (1986)

Acknowledgments

This book could not have been written, amidst the swirl of war and resistance to it, without my clever comrade Kevin Ovenden. My children, Sean and Lola, Lucy and Jay make life a joy. Yasmin Ataullah, my personal assistant, keeps me pointed in the right direction. My friends Brian Dempsey, Seumas Milne, Bob Wylie, John Boothman, John Rees, Lindsey German, John Bevan and Andrew Murray make sure I don't stray from the path. Ron McKay, my friend for 30 years is my rock. Rob Hoveman and Ayesha Bajwa make my office work. And the women I've loved and lost have all played their part in this story.

MQ Publications gave me the chance to write this book, for which I will always be grateful. But my deepest thanks must go to my friends in Cuba, particularly Teresita, Ricardo and Abel, and indeed to all the heroes of the Cuban Revolution, who have written the name of their country in the stars. I hope this book helps illustrate how luminous has been that story. In its light it is possible to see, as Nelson Mandela said on his first foreign journey after his release from the dungeons of apartheid, holding Fidel's hand aloft, "How far we slaves have come."

Unsurprisingly, I owe unparalleled thanks to the subject of this book, Fidel Castro, for, among many other things, making available his personal and Cuba's state archives, from which we selected the remarkable images that illustrate the book.

I wish also to thank all the people interviewed. They gave generously of their time and provided fresh and perceptive answers to my questions. In Cuba, thanks to Ricardo Alarcón, President of the National Assembly, Abel Prieto, Cuba's Minister of Culture and Comandante Ramiro Valdés. And thanks to Miguel Alvarez and Teresita Trujillo for making the interviews happen. In the U.S. I was fortunate to have the cooperation of Dr. Wayne S. Smith, José Pertierra and Alice Walker who all, in their different ways, have used their talents to fight for Cuba within, to use José Martí's phrase, "the entrails of the monster."

Many people in Cuba helped with the selection and preparation of the photographs. I thank in particular Pedro Alvarez Tabío, Director of the Office of Historical Affairs of the Council of State, and his comrades Elsa Montero and Efren González; Luis Enrique González, Director of the Prensa Latina press agency, and his comrades Iraida Rubí and Ismael Francisco; Delfín Xiqués, Director of Documentation at the national newspaper *Granma*; Lourdes Benigni, Director of Plastic Arts at Casa de Las Américas; and Hilda Barrio who was responsible for the research and documentation of the photographs.

Thanks also to all the photographers who through their fine work have helped to preserve the visual history of the Cuban Revolution. And to the authors of that history, to all those Cubans who left their blood and some their bones on the battlefield for freedom, I say:

Hasta la victoria siempre! Venceremos!

Dedication

To Fidel Castro,
a sprig of white heather in the future's lapel

Index

Page numbers in italics refer to captions

First published by MQ Publications Ltd
12 The Ivories
6–8 Northampton Street
London, N1 2HY
Tel: 020 7359 2244
Fax: 020 7359 1616
email: mail@mqpublications.com
website: www.mqpublications.com

North American Office:
49 West 24th Street, 8th Floor
New York, NY 10010
email: information@mqpublicationsus.com

ISBN: 1-84072-688-1
978-1-84072-688-6

10 9 8 7 6 5 4 3 2 1

Printed in France